the Hiking engine

A HIKER'S GUIDE TO THE CARE AND
MAINTENANCE OF FEET AND LEGS

BY STUART PLOTKIN, DPM

MENASHA RIDGE PRESS
Birmingham, Alabama

First edition, first printing
Published by Menasha Ridge Press
Distributed by The Globe Pequot Press

Library of Congress Cataloging-in-Publication Data

Plotkin, Stuart, 1953–
   The Hiking Engine: a hiker's guide to the care and
maintenance of feet and legs / by Stuart Plotkin.— 1st ed.
   p. cm.
   Including index.
   ISBN 0-89732-405-6
   1. Foot—Care and hygiene. 2. Leg—Care and hygiene.
3. Hiking injuries—Prevention. I. Title.

RD563 .P56 2001
617.5'85—dc21   2001044254

Photography by Stuart Plotkin, Menasha Ridge Press, and
   Limmer Boots, Inc.
Cover design by Grant Tatum
Text design by Ann Marie Healy
Illustrations by Chris Garrison

MENASHA RIDGE PRESS
P.O. Box 43673
Birmingham, AL 35243

www.menasharidge.com

Table of Contents

Note to Readers

This book was written to provide information and guidance concerning the proper care of the feet and legs in the context of hiking. It is not a substitute for proper medical care. Nor is this book a substitute for a proper first aid and CPR course. Health care information must be personalized to an individual's medical condition and circumstances. Consult your physician before starting an exercise program.

This book also has no agenda to endorse any particular trade-marked product. Products listed are not necessarily superior to others not listed; the products mentioned were selected simply as good representatives of a product type. When purchasing equipment, you should evaluate each product according to your own needs, preferences, and situation.

Every effort has been made to insure the accuracy of information within this work. However, products, businesses, and organizations may change, and medical research may lead to new recommendations while casting doubt on previously standard methods. Again, make sure to consult a physician before following any advice in this or any similar guidebook, and confirm that the information you find here is current for any product or practice you choose to employ.

Acknowledgments

I would like to thank my wife and daughter, Paula and Elyssa, for their confidence in me, as well as my parents. I would also like to thank Dr. Charles Levine, D.C., for his insights on the back, Ed Mitchelich for information on acupuncture, and Rosemarie Morawietz for her help on foot reflexology and massage. Thanks also to Dr. Preston Goforth and Phil Oren for lending their expertise. I especially want to thank my editor Bud Zehmer for his invaluable advice.

Preface

As an avid hiker and a health care provider, I naturally read many of the hiking-related medical texts on the market. I find them to be thorough about medical issues that rarely surface, yet surprisingly superficial about everyday injuries. After all, for every collapsed lung on the trail, there are probably a million blisters. I also note a lack of advice about preventive medicine. Many injuries are preventable, yet this information is missing in many texts.

As you read this book, you will notice an emphasis on prevention. You will also gain an appreciation of the beauty and complexity of the human gait and how the entire body acts synchronously when hiking. Of course, injuries do occur, and this book will teach you how to deal with problems on and off the trail. Equipment, training, stretching, and hikers with special needs are all discussed here—this work addresses the "meat and potatoes" of hiking.

—STUART PLOTKIN

The tendency nowadays to wander in the wilderness is delightful to see. Thousands of tired, nerve-shaken, overcivilized people are beginning to find out that going to the mountains is going home; that wildness is a necessity; and that mountain parks and reservations are useful not only as fountains of timber and irrigating rivers, but as fountains of life. Awakening from the stupefying effects of the vice of over-industry and the deadly apathy of luxury, they are trying the best they can to mix and enrich their own little ongoings with those of Nature, and to get rid of rust and disease. Briskly venturing and roaming, some are washing off sins and cobweb cares of the devil's spinning all day storms on mountains; sauntering in rosiny pinewoods or in gentian meadows, brushing through chaparral, bending down and parting sweet, flowery sprays; tracing rivers to their sources, getting in touch with the nerves of Mother Earth; jumping from rock to rock, feeling the life of them, learning the songs of them, panting in whole-souled exercise, and rejoicing in deep, long–drawn breaths of pure wilderness. So also is the growing interest in the care and preservation of forests and wild places.

—JOHN MUIR
1901

Introduction

Someone once said that everything is within walking distance if you have the time. And walk we do, seldom giving our feet and legs a second thought. We walk to and from our cars, do odd jobs around the house, and take after-dinner strolls, all by putting one foot in front of the other. It's no different if we want to get out into the great outdoors—cars and SUVs only get us so far. To reach our final destination, whether it's a mountain overlook or crashing waterfall, we depend on our feet and legs.

To veteran hikers, the benefits and rewards of hiking are well known. Not only does hiking keep our bodies fit, but it is important for our mental health as well—the beautiful scenery we encounter while hiking reduces stress, improving the quality of our sleep and helping alleviate depression. And as we age, it helps improve vitality, circulation, and keeps us "young at heart." As long as we don't start acting like mountain goats, it is one of the safest outdoor activities. In other words, with just a little common sense, some basic information, and the proper equipment, you can hike safely and comfortably any place you wish to explore. This is not to say hikers don't injure themselves. Occasionally they do.

A recent article published in the *Journal of the American Podiatric Medical Association* examined the risks and benefits of walking and hiking. The article stressed that benefits included weight control, increased bone calcium density (which helps prevent osteoporosis), lower cholesterol, increased sensitivity to insulin in diabetics, and a generally increased state of well-being. The article also included a study examining the types of injuries typically encountered by hikers.

In the study, the most common complaints of hikers (predictably) concerned their feet. These included arch pain, pain in the ball of the foot, and heel pain, all of which are overuse injuries (all are also easily treated). Problems with the legs included shin splints and Achilles tendonitis. Not surprisingly, knees were also prone to injury, especially when hiking hilly terrain (injuries also related to overuse). Interestingly, ankle sprains were actually more common in walkers than hikers, and problems generally associated with high-impact activities like running were not factors in hiking injuries.

In examining the nature of injuries associated with hikers, the article grouped injuries into four categories: accident, overuse, structural, and miscellaneous. Out of the 43 patients examined, the majority (80%) had injuries due to overuse. That is, people who pushed themselves a little too much past their limits or hiked just one mile too many before a break had a greater risk of hurting themselves than those who listened to their bodies and rested when necessary. What this means is that accidents are uncommon on the trail. The real pain comes from poor training, overdoing a hike, overestimating your ability, and, as we will discuss later, biomechanical problems such as flat feet.

So what can we learn from this study? Some accidents are truly just accidents, like stepping in a hole and spraining an ankle, but most hiking injuries can be prevented if we take care of ourselves and listen to our bodies.

This may be a good time to wax philosophic for a moment about the concept of safety. What is safe? Where is safe? What is acceptable risk? What isn't? Safety is subjective, which means individuals must answer these questions for themselves. Is it safe to live a life under the bed, so to speak? Is hiking safe? Can it be safer? Hiking **is** safe, but the degree of safety individuals are comfortable with differs from person to person. The best way to "push the envelope" is in small steps. As discussed in this book, we can and should take precautions. Stretching exercises are a good example of actively doing something to decrease risk. There is, however, an element of risk in everything; the best you can do is minimize risk without sacrificing a lifetime of experiences. Ultimately, only you can decide just how many risks you are comfortable with. Just as you should not take unnecessary risks, you should not allow theoretical risks rob you of positive experiences.

For those of us who regularly hike outdoors, a certain amount of discomfort is inevitable. Whose legs haven't complained after the second mile of a steep incline? But if we don't take care of our feet and legs, we may not reach our destination (or if we do arrive, we'll be in too much pain to enjoy it).

This book is named *The Hiking Engine* because the movement—or biomechanics—of hiking involves one interconnected system. Just as a car's engine requires that all its parts function properly together to move the car, our own body's joints, muscles, and bones form an interconnected system that must work in unison to propel us forward. But examining just the movement of our hiking engine is not enough. We also need to examine diet, fitness, training, stretching, and physical maintenance in order to get a more complete picture of how our body works to sustain itself. With this whole-body approach, we can better understand the mechanics of injuries and take steps to reduce and even prevent their occurrence.

As you read this book, you will find that prevention is the key to staying healthy on the trail. With some knowledge, good equipment, and proper care, you can prevent most injuries and minimize the effects of those that do occur. It doesn't matter whether you are taking a two-hour stroll around your local park or going on a month-long backpacking trip;

if you maintain your feet and legs (and your overall health and fitness), you can greatly reduce the possibility of discomfort (or disability) and enjoy a safe, comfortable trip. Ignore this idea, and the risk of discomfort and disability increases.

This book is broken down into several chapters that will first teach you a little bit about how feet and legs work and then how to keep them in good working order. So that we have a common understanding of biology and terminology, the first chapter examines the anatomy and biomechanics of the feet and legs. There will be no test at the end of the chapter, but you will learn how the bones and muscles of the hiking engine work together to propel us forward into the woods. After reading about our anatomy and "the way we work," you will gain insight into the beauty and marvel of human ambulation. The next chapter looks at the equipment available to the hiker: how to choose and fit gear and apparel, how to discern quality, and how to order specialty items such as orthotics. Then we'll look at preparation and maintenance of the hiking engine on and off the trail, which, in addition to the obligatory stretching before every hike, includes keeping in shape, eating properly, and staying hydrated. The next chapter examines hiking techniques—how to go uphill, downhill, across streams—as well as the special concerns of long-distance hikers. Finally, we'll look at how to treat the problems every hiker will eventually face. And because not every foot is created equal, we will examine common problems that are easily corrected yet keep many people from enjoying the outdoors.

While this book offers good advice for your feet and legs, it should not replace a medical evaluation and professional treatment. Any pre-existing problem or injury that **you** think is important enough to warrant seeking a doctor's advice **is** important enough—make it so! This book will greatly aid you in increasing your comfort level when hiking, but your own judgement must prevail in seeking medical care. Also, do yourself and your buddies a lifesaving favor and take a CPR and first aid course from your local Red Cross. Hopefully, you will never need that information—but if you do, it will be a lifesaver.

Hiking is a physical and mental challenge and therefore great for self-confidence. When you make it to the top of a mountain, to an isolated waterfall, or even through your local park, you feel good about yourself, you accomplish a goal, and your confidence soars. Whether you hike with groups or by yourself, *The Hiking Engine* will help you have safer and more pleasant experiences in the outdoors.

Close your eyes and picture a warm autumn day. You are hiking in a park; the sun is shining, and it's 68°; the blue sky is dotted with white fluffy clouds; the leaves on nearby oak and maple trees range in color from dark green to yellow, orange, red, and brown; you smell the aromas of pine and musty leaf mold; you hear bird calls, a few crickets, and perhaps a small chipmunk running through the underbrush. You also hear the far-off sound of rushing water. As you walk, the sound gets louder and the sun starts backlighting the leaves, making them glow. The trail takes you to a fast-moving stream, which plunges 100 feet, cascading over broken rocks. Feel your body—heart pumping smoothly—gliding effortlessly down the trail. Your excitement and exhilaration rise as the waterfall comes into view.

Now feel free to imagine some of the hikes **you** have been on—all the sights, sounds, smells, and experiences. Have you ever felt better? Was it worth the effort? You bet it was.

Happy hiking!

Anatomy and Biomechanics
HOW THE HIKING ENGINE WORKS

Just as you don't need to under-
stand how a combustion engine works to get in your car and drive, you
don't need to understand the workings of your muscles and bones to go
hiking. However, even a passing familiarity with the biomechanics of
walking will make you more aware of every step—and hopefully more
careful, thus putting you on the road toward injury prevention. Read-
ers wishing simply to get to the nuts and bolts of foot care may want
to skip this chapter for now. You may, however, want to return, since
later chapters refer to terms discussed here.

TERMINOLOGY

It will do us both good to get some terminology straight, so that
when I say that the anterior tibial muscle is located just lateral to the
shin bone and dorsiflexes the foot, you'll know what I'm talking
about. I promise you I won't get quite that technical in the text, but
knowing the terms for the underlying structures of the feet and legs
(the bones, sinews and muscles, or in other words our **anatomy**) as
well as how these structures move in order to propel us gracefully forward (also known as **biomechanics**) will be invaluable to understanding the rest of this book as well as offering insight as to how some
injuries occur.

7

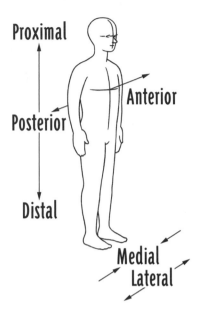

The first set of terms identifies location in the body, allowing us to determine where an anatomical feature is in relation to the body as a whole as well as other anatomical elements. For instance, features that are toward the head are said to be **proximal,** while those items toward the feet are called **distal.** For example, the knee is distal to the hip and proximal to the foot. We can also describe whether a body part is toward the front or toward the back of the body: **anterior** and **posterior,** respectively. Kneecaps are anterior, whereas heels are posterior. Finally, we can describe whether a feature lies toward the center of the body, **medial,** or toward the outside, **lateral.** For example, the big toe is medial, and the pinky toe is lateral.

Viewed another way, this terminology provides a three-dimensional grid of the body, providing descriptions for up and down (proximal and distal), front to back (anterior and posterior), and side to side (medial and lateral).

Now that we know how to describe location, we need some terms that describe movement. Most of these you probably already know. If we straighten out a joint, we are **extending** it, while when we bend a joint, we are usually **flexing** it. For example, bending your elbow is flexing, straightening your knee extending. There is also specific terminology for moving the foot around. If the foot moves up at the ankle joint, it is **dorsiflexing,** and if it moves down, it is **plantarflexing;** or said another way, if you stand on your toes, your foot is plantarflexing, and if you raise your toes above your heels, your foot is dorsiflexing.

ANATOMY AND BIOMECHANICS

When people think about anatomy, the image that probably first comes to mind is of the skeleton that always hung out in the corner of their high school biology class. Anatomy is certainly about bones, but it also encompasses the ligaments and sinews that tie those bones together, not to mention the muscles and tendons that move those bones, the nerves that command them, and the blood vessels that circulate blood. **Bones** are living tissue—their shape and strength are remodeled constantly due to the pressures put on them. They are obviously the framework for our body. **Tendons** attach muscles to bone. They are very strong fibrous bands, but they do not have the best blood supply, so they tend to heal slowly. A good example is the Achilles tendon, which attaches the powerful calf muscle to the back of the heel. **Ligaments** attach bones to bones across a joint. They help stabilize joints, preventing them from moving further than they should, thereby preventing injury. For example, ligaments attach the small leg bone (fibula) to the heel bone (calcaneus) across the ankle joint. These ligaments are commonly injured in an ankle sprain.

Those are the basics, but don't worry about a full-blown anatomy lesson here. We're only going to look at a very narrow section of our anatomy—generally those parts that directly concern hikers.

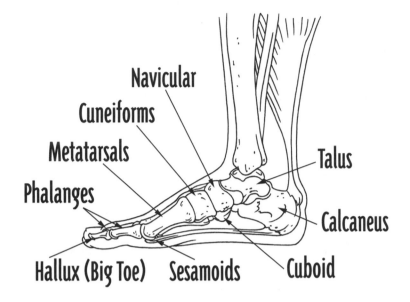

As I mentioned earlier, anatomy is only part of the picture. To see how all the parts of the body interact with each other (at least the muscles and bones), we need to look at the biomechanics. Simply put, biomechanics is the science of movement, or how bones, joints, ligaments, tendons, and muscles come together to allow us to move gracefully through space.

THE FOOT

The foot is a remarkable device. It must walk over 100,000 miles in a lifetime, adjust to irregular surfaces, get stuffed into ill-fitting shoes, and take decades of abuse. Its job is to take us where we want to go. It's where we make contact with our environment—where the "pedal hits the metal," so to speak. The foot has 26 bones, dozens of joints, tendons, 100 ligaments, nerves, blood vessels, and even specialized skin. (The bottom of the foot has no hair, no oil glands, and special sweat glands to aid in traction.)

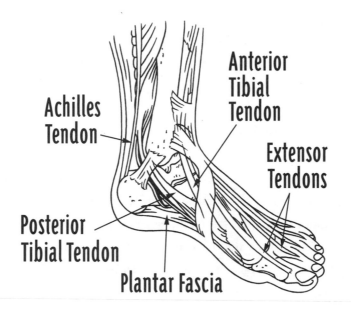

Achilles Tendon

Anterior Tibial Tendon

Extensor Tendons

Posterior Tibial Tendon

Plantar Fascia

When looking at the skeletal structure of the foot from anterior to posterior, the first bones we encounter are the **phalanges,** or toe bones, which comprise 14 of the 26 bones in the foot. One in particular has a special name—the **hallux.** Most people call it the big toe. The others, alas, are nameless (a possible job for a future anatomist). Behind these are the five **metatarsals,** which form the ball of the foot. The first of these metatarsals is medial to and much beefier than the other four; beneath it are two pea-shaped bones called **sesamoids.** These bones act as a fulcrum (similar in function to the kneecap) for the tendon that helps the hallux move. The next set of bones we encounter make up the midfoot. These form the arch of our foot and consist of the **navicular, cuneiforms,** and the **cuboid.** The heel bone is the **calcaneus.** The last foot bone, the **talus,** is proximal to the rest (nearer the head) and connects the foot and the leg, and is part of a critical joint called the **subtalar** joint (STJ). The talus is locked into the ankle by the ends of the tibia and fibula.

Tying the foot together are numerous ligaments and tendons. Surprisingly, foot muscles only act as stabilizers for the bones and tendons. Muscles originating in the lower leg are really the main movers of the foot. These muscles, attached to the many tendons threading throughout the foot, do the actual flexing and extending.

The ligaments of the foot hold its joints together. The most important ligaments to hikers are the ankle ligaments—the ones most often sprained. Remember, a ligament's job is to stabilize a joint and stop it from moving past its normal range of motion. Another important structure is called the **plantar fascia.** Although not exactly a ligament, it is a strong fibrous band that runs from the heel bone forward into the toes. A major stabilizer of the arch, the plantar fascia is discussed in great length in the section on heel spurs and plantar fasciitis. You can actually see and feel the plantar fascia in your foot. While looking at the bottom of your foot, pull up on your big toe. In the medial arch, you will see the tightening edge of the plantar fascia.

Biomechanics of the Foot

As always in the design of our bodies, there is a good reason why we have so many bones in our feet. These bones permit the foot to be very flexible, essentially allowing the foot to mold itself around the uneven terrain it encounters as we walk. As we take a step, the individual foot bones move up or down in relation to one another as they seek good purchase on the ground. But the most important movement of the foot, the one crucial to understanding why things go wrong with our feet, involves two joints: the **ankle joint** and the **subtalar joint** (STJ).

The ankle joint itself is only responsible for the up and down motion of the foot, allowing the foot to dorsiflex and plantarflex. Located just below the ankle, the STJ is the pivotal joint in the leg, connecting the foot to the leg, knee, and hip, and is responsible for the side-to-side motion of the foot. Without these two joints, we would walk around like Frankenstein, lurching from step to step.

The STJ allows the foot to adapt to irregular terrain, helps absorb shock, and aids in normal knee rotation; it does this by allowing the foot to **pronate** and **supinate.** As you take a step and your heel first contacts the ground, your foot is pronating at the STJ. This motion causes the arch height to decrease or flatten out. Pronating thus relaxes the foot and allows more surface area to touch the ground, permitting the foot to adjust to irregular terrain for better stability and traction. As the body moves over the planted foot, it supinates. This turns the foot into a rigid lever which propels the body forward. The process starts all over again with the next step.

If you want to see pronation and supination in action, sit down and try the following. In order to pronate your foot, try moving it up, rotate it out, and turn the bottom of your foot away from the midline of the body. You will notice the arch lower, and the foot become more flexible. To supinate your foot, do the reverse. Move it down, rotate in inward, and turn the bottom of the foot towards the midline of the body. Now the arch height increases, and the foot becomes more rigid.

Some people may have problems with supination and pronation. For many it's a matter of timing. For example, a flat-footed person's foot hits the ground pronated, but it either resupinates late, or not at all. This foot never gets its act together, and walking becomes inefficient and unstable. As a result, symptoms like bunions, hammertoes, and heel spurs can develop. It is not a question of one movement being "good" and one "bad" but a question of timing. In order to have a smooth and energy-efficient stride, the entire gait cycle depends on the foot pronating and supinating at the correct time

As you will see, what goes on above the leg greatly influences foot biomechanics. Having "bowlegs," "knock-knees," "pigeon toes," or legs

There are three basic foot types: the rare person with a "normal" foot, the low-arch flat foot, and the high-arch cavus foot. There is actually more of a spectrum, with the low arch on one end, high arch on the other, and most people's feet falling somewhere in between. It is the feet that lean toward either extreme that produce problems. It is important to realize that muscles do not support the arch. Arch height is determined by the shapes of bones in a foot, kind of like an interlocking puzzle.

People with flat feet can have problems with excess pronation, which makes the foot function like a "loose bag of bones," creating a weak, unstable foot. This condition can cause the knee to shift to the inside (a common cause of "runner's knee" or Chondromalacia Patella Syndrome). Flat feet can develop bunions, hammertoes, heel spurs, arthritis, and cause knee, hip, and back pain. Flat feet need as much support as they can get, but note that not all need medical treatment or special care.

People with high arches can have unstable footing too, but for different reasons. Instead of a bag of bones, high arches create a rigid foot, which can be easily toppled by a small rut in the ground. Cavus feet also have limited shock-absorbing ability, causing a variety of leg, back, and neck pain. The heel can hurt from the constant pounding and the toes often claw up. Because it can't pronate enough, a high-arch foot has a limited ability to compensate for uneven terrain, and it does not take much force to cause the ankle to roll over, potentially causing ligament damage. A cavus foot likes as much cushioning as it can get.

How can you tell if you have a high, normal, or low arch? You can see a podiatrist, or take a wet-foot imprint or sand imprint. You must be standing to determine your arch height. Your foot may look very different when your are seated than it does when bearing your full weight.

of different lengths will affect the way a person's foot hits the ground. The foot then has to compensate for these structural problems, and it is this compensation that causes symptoms. "Bowlegs" are a good example. This is a common structural curving of the tibia. Imagine you have a five-degree bowing of your lower leg. This means your foot hits the ground five degrees inverted. So unless you want to walk around on your fifth toe, you must pronate your entire foot to get the hallux to the ground. This excess pronation is the cause of chronic foot and leg pain.

THE LEG

Once we leave the foot behind, we have fewer bones to worry about—four actually. As we work up the leg, we encounter the main bone in the lower leg, the **tibia**, and the thinner bone on the lateral side of the lower leg, the **fibula.** Both lock in the talus joint on either side of the ankle, and then proceed up to the knee. Bones are said to **articulate** when they meet at a joint. The tibia articulates with the femur, or thigh bone, at the knee joint, while the fibula articulates just below the knee on the lateral side. You can feel the head of the fibula just below the knee joint. In fact, there is a nerve running there that if you bang accidentally will hurt like the funny bone in your elbow. Continuing up the leg (we'll return to the knee in a moment), we reach one of the strongest and largest bones in the body, the **femur;** it articulates at the knee and the hip.

Biomechanics of the Leg

Though the muscles in the leg do their share of stabilizing, they are also the movers and shakers of our bodies. In the lower leg there are four main groups.

The **extensor group** is comprised of the **anterior tibial** muscle (the chief dorsiflexor of the foot and one of the shin splint muscles) and the **toe extensors.** These muscles are important in controlling how

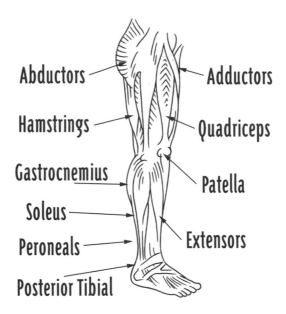

Abductors

Adductors

Hamstrings

Quadriceps

Gastrocnemius

Patella

Soleus

Peroneals

Extensors

Posterior Tibial

the foot hits the ground. They are commonly overused going downhill. If they are relatively weak, shin splints develop. Bad cases can lead to tibial stress fractures.

The second group makes up the powerful **gastrocnemius** and **soleus** muscles. These are the chief plantarflexing muscles. The primary calf muscle, the gastrocnemius starts at the Achilles tendon in the heel, goes up the calf, crosses the hamstring tendons (described below), and ultimately attaches behind and above the knee on the femur. Because both the hamstrings and "gastroc" muscles cross the knee, both affect knee function. A tight calf muscle creates a strong pronating, or foot- flattening force, causing a whole slew of foot problems, including heel spurs and arch pain. The soleus muscle is also part of the Achilles tendon, but it starts below the knee. This muscle helps stabilize the foot on the floor and supinates the STJ.

The third group, the **peroneals,** are located on the lateral part of the leg and act as stabilizers to the foot. Part of this group attaches to the fifth metatarsal; the other dives deep into the foot and crosses to the first metatarsal. These latter peroneals are vital for stabilizing the big toe joint. They are both pronators and everters of the STJ. (Everters rotate the foot outward, and inverters rotate the foot inwards.)

The fourth and last is the **posterior tibial** muscle, located on the medial side of the lower leg, under the "gastroc-soleus" muscle group. This is the second shin splint muscle, and one of its jobs is to support the arch. It inverts and supinates the STJ.

There are also four major muscle groups in the thigh. The first group is the **quadriceps,** so named because these four distinct muscles join at the **patella** (or kneecap) tendon. The quadriceps is one of the strongest muscle groups in the body. It crosses both the hip and the knee joint, enabling it to flex the hip and extend the knee. The quadriceps also stabilize and control the gliding of the patella in its proper tract. An imbalance between the medial and lateral muscles of the quadriceps can cause a patella mal-alignment—if the kneecap doesn't track in the groove in the femur, one develops runner's knee, or Chondromalacia Patella Syndrome (described below).

The second group, the **hamstrings,** make up the back of the thigh. The powerful hamstrings, actually three muscles, attach to the pelvis and cross the knee, with two attaching behind the medial knee and the other to the lateral knee. If they are too tight, they force you to walk with your knees slightly bent at all times, a fatiguing and troublesome gait. This is a common occurrence in hikers and requires stretching.

The third group, the **adductor** muscles, is found in the medial thigh and includes the groin muscles.

The fourth group, the **abductor** muscles, is very important to hikers, especially when hiking uphill, but they are seldom injured while hiking. These are the buttocks muscles, including the **gluteus maximus.** They are "antigravity muscles" that keep you upright when standing still. The gluteus maximus really comes into its own climbing up hills. After advancing your leg up, its job is to pull the rest of your body up.

THE KNEE

While the hip and ankle joints are well stabilized by the structure of the bones meeting there, the knee joint is quite vulnerable to injury. Its job of being flexible enough to move yet sturdy enough to bear the entire body's weight puts it in a difficult position. The knee is stabilized by the muscles and ligaments around it as well as its internal cruciate ligaments, the ones the football players constantly tear. Not only do the bones of the knee fail to support the joint, they do not exactly match, so a shock absorber is built into the joint—the **menisci.** These fibrous rings inside the knee help reduce shock and improve alignment. Cap this off with a kneecap that is supposed to glide in a groove in the femur to improve the mechanical advantage of the quadriceps, and you have a joint trying to be stable and flexible at the same time—an engineering nightmare. Evolutionarily, I think it is still a work in progress. For now, let's briefly consider the structures involved in three common knee injuries.

The **patella,** or kneecap, acts like a fulcrum, giving the quadriceps, the major thigh-muscle group, a better mechanical advantage in moving us around. That is why an imbalance between the medial and lateral muscles of the quadriceps can cause a patella mal-alignment, which spells trouble for the hiker. If the patella doesn't track properly in its groove, over time the cartilage erodes, the knee has a crumbly feeling, pain develops, and Chondromalacia ensues.

Another important structure of the knee is the **iliotibial band.** You can feel this band by rubbing your fingers on the lateral side of an extended leg. It feels like a tight cord. This thick band of tissue extends from the thigh down over the knee and attaches to the tibia. When the

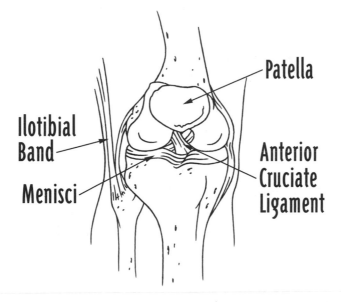

Patella

Ilotibial Band

Menisci

Anterior Cruciate Ligament

knee bends and straightens, the iliotibial band slides over the bony prominences of the outer knee. Friction here causes chronic pain in some hikers.

If you have spent any time around active people, you've probably heard of ACL surgery. This refers to the **anterior cruciate ligament**, the most commonly damaged ligament in the knee. There are two **cruciate** ligaments that lie within the knee joint, and both greatly add to the stability of the knee. One tightens when the knee is flexed, the other tightens when the knee is extended. If these ligaments are torn, the knee becomes unstable and often requires arthroscopic surgery. Just ask any football player.

THE HIP AND LOWER BACK

There are a great many other important muscles and ligaments throughout the body, but here are the more commonly injured sites for hikers. The hip joint is a sturdy ball and socket joint that supports the entire upper body. There are powerful muscles that surround the hip including the **gluteal** muscle group. The lower back muscles include the **quadratus, lumborum,** and **erector spinae** (those commonly strained in hiking with packs).

The only points I want to make about the spine concern its relationship with the legs. It is, of course, the origin of all the nerves that enter the leg. A pinched nerve or a disc problem can send shooting pains into the leg, causing numbness and muscle weakness. Scoliosis can produce an apparent difference in limb length. Sometimes you may need to address this with a heel lift—but other times a lift may actually worsen the scoliosis, so do not attempt self-treatment. Contact your physician or chiropractor.

Equipment
OUTFITTING THE HIKING ENGINE

It's no accident that several of the mainstream outdoor magazines devote an issue each year to examining the many iterations of camping and hiking gear. Though the rate of technological change doesn't compare to what's found in the computer industry, the number of new materials and technologies appearing each year quickly make the cutting-edge equipment of just five years ago seem out-of-date. Stepping into a store can lead to confusion, especially when, other than style, there appears to be little substantial difference between one piece of equipment or clothing and another.

The good news is that you do not need to have the latest in boot and sock technology to hike safely and comfortably. Everything you read in this book will help you have an enjoyable and safe trip, whether your hiking outfit involves wool socks and leather boots or Coolmax socks and lightweight, synthetic boots. Keep in mind that there is no single perfect piece of equipment. Each has advantages and disadvantages, depending on your intended activity as well as how your body is made. But the following will help you make informed decisions and offers guidelines that will apply to whatever future technologies crop up.

This chapter starts with the foundation of hiking equipment—socks and boots—then examines other equipment needs and concerns that can help prevent a painful hiking experience.

Socks

There are few things more important on a hike than your socks. Good socks will greatly reduce the probability of blisters, cushion the constant pounding experienced by hiking feet, and, when the weather is inclement, keep them warm. But how to choose? Socks come in a bewildering array of materials, not to mention shapes, sizes, and colors. Unfortunately, you can't determine how a sock will perform by just looking at one—nothing beats a test drive—but there are two things you should consider before plopping your money down: what are the socks made of, and how are they constructed?

Also keep in mind that a major concern with any sock is how well it keeps your foot dry. Wet feet are more prone to blister, in addition to being potentially cold and uncomfortable. This challenge can vary according to temperature, hiking conditions, weather, and more. Note that many socks are classified as either hydrophilic or hydrophobic. **Hydrophilic** socks (most natural fibers, like wool) wick moisture away from the foot, while **hydrophobic** socks (most synthetic fibers, like polyester) use heat to transfer moisture away from the foot via capillary action.

MATERIALS

Wool was the standard sock material for generations of outdoor adventurers, and in spite of the many advances in textiles, it is still the choice for many hikers. Its chief advantage is its ability to absorb water without feeling wet. Wool can absorb up to 30 percent of its weight in moisture before it begins to feel damp.

Generations of hikers have also used cotton, much to their misfortune. Because cotton absorbs water and feels damp immediately, holding moisture on the skin rather than taking it away, it aids in keeping the body cool—an advantage when you're working out in a hot gym. However, for hikers, wet cotton is certain to induce painful blisters,

Hiking socks come in a wide variety of styles, materials, weights, and padding.

and in cold weather, cotton-clad feet can quickly turn into ice cubes. Between the two, wool is the obvious choice.

So, is wool the right choice overall? Like so many things in life, that depends... Wool is cheaper than some of the blend alternatives available, though some poorly-made wool socks wear out quickly in the heel and have a tendency to droop down into your boot, potentially causing blisters. Finer grades of wool will wear out more quickly than coarser grades. Also, some people don't like the smell of wet wool, or they find it annoyingly itchy. A special type of wool that avoids many of wool's itchy qualities—merino wool—comes from a particular type of sheep. If you do find most wool socks irritating, try socks made with merino wool, or look for it blended with other materials. Smartwool, a combination of merino wool and nylon as well as other proprietary materials, is another good option.

Another natural material is silk, which is often used as a blend with other materials. Primarily available as a liner, silk feels quite nice against the skin, and it isn't bulky—it provides a good amount of warmth for its weight. Silk hydrophilic socks have a low friction factor, high abrasion resistance, and are soft, absorbent, and good for people with allergies to wool and synthetic socks. However, silk tends to be more expensive and requires a lot more care than wool.

Given technological advances in textiles, it is now quite unusual to find a sock made of entirely one material. Most are made from blends of many materials, natural and synthetic, combining the best properties of each. Some of the materials, like spandex, prevent socks from falling around your ankles, while others—olefin, acrylic, and nylon—add durability as well as help a sock retain its shape.

One of the first groundbreaking synthetic materials for outdoor enthusiasts was polypropylene. It was durable, and like wool, it kept you warm when wet, but it had two drawbacks. Polypro, as it was known, retained body odor, and if it found its way into a hot dryer, it shrank. Both of these problems, particularly odor retention, have been somewhat alleviated by more advanced polypro blends. You can still find polypro socks (mainly as sock liners), but they have mostly given way to more advanced proprietary materials, such as Capilene, Coolmax, and Thermax. Each makes claims of fabulous wicking power. Whether one works better than the others is a matter of personal opinion, but you probably won't go wrong with a sock made with these materials. You will find that the ideal sock is a mixture of materials, one for warmth, one for wicking and breathability, one for elasticity and to hold shape, and one for cushioning.

There is a new generation of synthetic fabrics that claim to have a certain amount of "intelligence" in keeping our feet warm. These fabrics react to the temperature around them, absorbing or dissipating heat, depending on the circumstances. These proprietary materials include Outlast and ComfortTemp DCC. Manufacturers claim that each will release heat slowly, keeping the feet warm after the hike has ended. This is something for cold-weather hikers to consider.

CONSTRUCTION

Using the right kind of material in a sock doesn't mean a thing unless the sock is put together well. A well-constructed sock will improve a boot's fit, reduce the shearing forces that cause blisters, and demonstrate durability over time. And it will feel snug and comfortable. The following are a few things to look for when evaluating whether or not a sock is constructed well and whether or not it is the best sock for your hiking style.

Before purchasing the socks, turn them inside out to inspect the seams, their thickness, and the mix of materials. Most socks have seams, but the cheap ones will have thick irritating seams, especially around the toes. These seams absorb rather than wick away sweat and can create a rather unpleasant trail experience. Diabetics and those with sensitive feet should consider seamless socks. Companies such as Knit-Rite have a seamless sock made with Coolmax, antifungal-impregnated fibers, and a nonrestrictive elastic top to prevent slipping. Lin socks have a more advanced toe-seam closure with no excessive seam thickness.

Your next concern should be how thoroughly the sock is padded. The ball/heel of the sock should have adequate padding in order to absorb the constant pounding associated with hiking. Thor-Lo is famous for making hiking socks with extra padding in the ball and heel area. These are probably the most cushioned socks on the market. If you have a tendency to get blisters on your Achilles tendon, extra padding here will help (as well as extend the life of the sock). Note, however, that all padding is not created equal—more terry loops per square inch (usually described as high stitch density) equals more comfort.

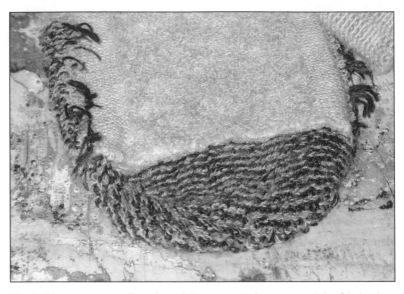

The inside seam on a well-made sock is constructed to cause minimal irritation.

Those of us who have had to constantly pull up the top of a pair of socks know that is potentially the most annoying result of ill-fitting socks. You want to make sure that the top of the sock is snug enough so that it won't droop down—this could lead to the whole sock bunching up in your boot and giving you blisters. Cheap socks are notorious for this—that's why a high-performance, well-made, fitted sock is a good idea if you're doing serious hiking.

The length of a sock is another matter of personal taste. Socks should, however, come up over the ankle and past the boot top. Calf-length socks help protect your legs from insects, stinging nettles, and stray branches hitting your shin, and to a lesser degree, they may retard muscle fatigue. These socks do support the veins a bit, but if you truly have a vein problem, then support hose are a better idea.

Finally, the toe area of a sock should have adequate room to prevent your toes from squishing together and allow your toes, generally a very sweaty area, to breathe.

Clearly, the season you hike in strongly impacts your decision on which sock to wear. You don't want to wear a heavy-duty sock in the middle of summer—if your feet are too hot, your sweat can translate into a nice-sized blister. Even the best socks can't keep up with a profusely sweating foot.

Once you have chosen a sock, make sure that it compliments your boot fit. You don't want a sock that will be too snug—over the course of a day of hiking, your circulation can be reduced, causing problems such as cold feet. Most people err on the other side of the equation and end up wearing socks that are too big, which can result in discomfort and blistering as the sock migrates around the heel and bunches up.

SOCK LINERS

Some people find one sock does the job, others swear by using layers—a very thin sock liner that helps to wick away moisture covered by a thicker outer sock that provides warmth and cushioning. Liners can also help prevent blisters and calluses. It comes down to a matter of personal preference. Some manufacturers make a "double-layer" sock that (as its name implies) has two layers: an inner lining of either Coolmax or Thermolite (previously known as Thermastat) and an outer layer of acrylic and wool. I recommend you experiment with sock liners; you may like them.

FOOT WARMERS

For cold-weather hiking, various foot-warming devices and chemical packets are available from different manufacturers. It is unlikely that you will need these for most winter trips because your feet generate a great deal of heat when walking. There may be times, however, when they are of great help: in the evenings when camping, for example. (A warning for diabetics and other patients with diminished sensation to their feet. It is possible to get a burn from warming devices. Unable to feel this occurring, the diabetic is at risk of injury.)

BOOTS

Besides socks, boots are the most important piece of hiking equipment you will buy. Boots shelter, support, and protect your feet from the many elements you encounter while hiking. But they have a hard time doing all this if they do not fit well. Buying a pair of boots can be quite daunting; you don't want to plop down a lot of money only to have your boots turn against you. However, buying boots is probably a lot easier than you imagine.

I know what you want! You want the name of the perfect boot for your own personal feet. As much as I'd like to oblige you, I'm afraid that's just not possible. Every foot is unique and has its own needs. But what I can do is give you some advice. Rest assured, there are many fine boot companies out there (just turn to the appendix and you'll find contacts for most of them). And by the way, even when searching for a boot to buy, don't hike in someone else's boot. Their boots will have warped to fit their own style of walking, which could throw off your own biomechanics and cause serious injury. In other words, "Don't walk in another man's shoes!"

Below you'll find a brief primer on how boots are put together, and then more importantly, how to choose the best boot for your needs.

PARTS OF THE BOOT

The outside and most visible part of the boot is the **upper.** The upper can be made of leather, nylon, synthetics, or a combination. You will notice that most medium- to heavyweight boots will have all leather uppers, though there are some exceptions. Full-grain leather uppers are

Your knowledge of how a boot is manufactured will probably not be the deciding factor when buying a particular boot, but it should give you some insight into the durability of different boots—and why one size 8 fits differently than another.

To make boots, manufacturers need a model to build the boots around so that every time a particular size is created, it will match all others of that size. This model is called a "last," and is based on an actual human being's foot. Some person has the perfect-shape size 8 (or 9 or 10) foot and these lasts are created to match the size and shape of that person's feet. Lasts are made of wood, and they represent the manufacturer's concept of the average foot for any given size. There is a last for every shoe size, of every width, for every boot style. These lasts are one of the manufacturer's most precious secrets, and that is why a size 8 boot from Merrel is not the same as a size 8 from Vasque.

How does knowing that help you? First, don't be hung up on a particular size. So you normally where a size 8 sneaker? Start there, but don't be afraid to go up or down a half or even a full size in order to get the best fit. You also should try boots by different manufacturers—not only do sizes differ between different manufacturers, but shapes can differ quite a bit too, and you may find a better match for your own foot shape, insuring a better fit.

You may encounter the terms **board last, slip last,** and **combination last.** These terms refer to the way the boot is constructed and not the last itself. Shoes constructed using a board last method are more rigid and better for overpronators. A slip last construction gives a boot more flexibility—better for a rigid high arch foot. As you can guess, a combination last is a compromise between the two.

Boot lasts at the Limmer Boot factory.

tough, water-resistant, and, because they are generally made of one piece, reduce the chance of leakage—fewer seams, fewer leaks. Their main drawback is that they tend to be heavy and stiff, requiring a significant break-in period. There are some all-leather boots that are made from several pieces of stitched leather, and as long as you keep the seams waterproof, these are a good alternative. Boot leathers come in varying thicknesses: 3.2 mm leathers are found on heavy, sturdy boots; midweight boot leathers are between 2.4 and 2.8 mm; and lightweight boots may have split-leather uppers from 1.6 to 1.8 mm thick.

Uppers made of synthetic material are lightweight and tend to be more flexible. They also need a waterproof coating to make them water resistant, which can wear off.

A combination of leather and nylon may be suitable for most hikers, since it combines the best of both worlds—the durability of leather and the lighter weight of the synthetics.

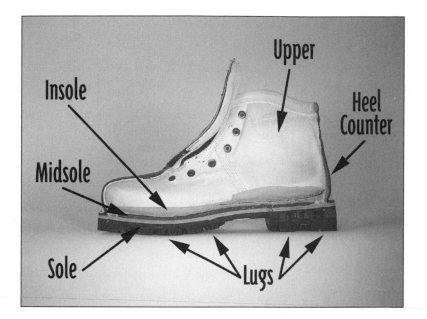

The **heel counter** is another critical aspect of boots. This is the part of the upper boot directly behind the heel. Its job is to hold the heel as vertical as possible. To accomplish this, the heel counter must be rigid and have an inner layer of reinforcing plastic or leather. If you wear orthotics, you especially need a sturdy heel counter. Also keep in mind that if you kick your boots off without undoing the laces, you will quickly break down the heel counter, making the boots useless. When the heel counter of your boot softens up, it is time for a new boot.

The upper is sewn or glued to the **midsole,** which supports your foot. Though some people swear by sewn boots, contemporary glues are as reliable as stitching. The midsole is made of various densities of foam and rubber. As nice as soft foam sounds, it quickly flattens out, reducing its ability to act as a shock absorber. When shopping for a boot, make sure the midsole is made of resilient materials. For mid- and heavyweight boots, the midsole is stiffened with either a steel or plastic shank. This protects the foot from sharp rocks and gives added stability over rough terrain. The shank also affects the torsional motion of the boot. This is the ability of the boot to twist. A flat-footed overpronator should look for a more rigid shank, allowing less twisting motion. A high-arched foot supinator should get a more flexible shank. These considerations, more than your intended hiking terrain, may influence your boot-buying decision.

Below the midsole is the **sole** of the boot. Most soles are made of Vibram or some other rubber and all have **lugs** on them that help your foot grip the trail. The lug pattern is not as important a consideration as the depth of the lugs. Deep lugs are needed for grip on tougher trails but cause more damage to the trail surface, while shallower lugs are easier on the environment. A sole's grip also has a lot to do with the type of rubber used. Softer rubber bottoms will give you more grip, but wear more quickly; while tougher, long-lasting rubber may not always grip as well, but it will last a long time.

There are a few useful options available on many boots that you may want to consider. For instance, how would you like your boots to secure (i.e. lace-up or close)? Some boots offer Velcro closures, while others have d-ring or quick-lace system. Velcro is found more on running shoe–type lightweight boots, and is not to be used as a primary closure on a mid- or heavyweight boot. Presently all good boots have some type of speed lace system—it took just too long to lace up the old way. Also, you should consider whether you want a "waterproof" boot or not—plenty of boots are made with a Goretex liner, a durable water-repellant fabric that beads up water on the outside but lets perspiration pass through. When shopping for boots, it is important to look at the boot's padding around the Achilles tendon. This is a common place for blisters and should be examined to make sure it is sufficiently padded. Finally, make sure the insole (the part your foot rests on) can be easily removed for replacement or for orthotics if you wear them; between your body weight and perhaps a hefty pack, the insoles of a boot wear fast. They are often soft pieces of foam that bottom-out quickly and need replacement at least every six months.

CHOOSING THE RIGHT BOOT

Before you head to the store to buy boots, you should consider a few things first. Primarily, what kind of hiking are you going to do? Do you plan to take the occasional weekend camping trip and go for short hikes? Or maybe you plan on taking a lot of week-long trips. Perhaps you're planning a three-month journey along the Pacific Crest Trail? The frequency of your outings and difficulty of the terrain should definitely influence your decision.

The more intense your hiking or the greater your load, the heavier your boot should be. Traditionally, boots have been categorized according to their weight, and many backpacking books still describe them that way. But look at a boot catalog, and won't often see a boot listed as lightweight or heavy. Manufacturers now use descriptions that relate to a boot's appropriate activity. For example, you'll probably see boots listed as appropriate for approach hikes, day hikes, hiking or trekking, or backpacking. You still have the range of boot weight, from approach shoes (basically revved-up tennis shoes) to backpacking boots (the all-leather, heavy-duty kind).

So, should you buy light- or heavyweight boots? There are people who go on extended hikes that swear by lightweight boots, and there are those who hike two or three times a year that have boots capable of assaulting Mount Everest. Ultimately it's up to you to choose, but let's first look at the advantages that boots of different weights offer the hiker, and then you can decide.

Approach boots or shoes are the most lightweight shoes you can buy. Basically a muscled- up running shoe, they generally weigh in at about one pound, but there are some heavier ones that have higher uppers to

Limmer ultra-lightweight hiking boot.

give added ankle protection. Generally, approach boots have great shock absorption but do not support the ankle. They are best for well-groomed trails that are relatively smooth, and if you are willing to carry the extra load, they're great to put on in camp at the end of the day.

Boots labeled as appropriate for day hikes are traditional light-weight boots. They are mostly made of synthetic materials and general-ly weigh in between one and two pounds. They get wet easily but also dry quickly. The upper may not come to the ankle, so like the approach shoes, they offer limited support . They rarely need breaking in and are appropriate for somewhat-rocky trails in fair weather. Their treads are often not very deep. If they have a shank, it isn't very long, allowing for greater flexibility in the boot.

If you plan to go on more extended trips or hike on trails that en-tail some rock scrambling, you may consider a hiking or trekking boot. These often have a 3/4 length steel shank that helps prevent bruising when you step on sharp rocks, and their uppers come up above the

Limmer midweight hiking boot.

ankle. They have a deep lug tread for traction. They are also generally leather or a blend of leather and synthetics, and can weigh between one and one-half and three pounds. While heavier, these boots support the ankle and protect the bottom of the foot from sharp rocks.

It should go without saying, but carrying a heavy load affects your feet. The more weight you carry, the harder your feet are punched into the ground. Without proper support, you could sustain an injury. Heavyweight boots, referred to as backpacking boots, are generally made of all leather and are very stiff, giving the ultimate in support. They also take a long time to break in, but as long as your take care of them, you'll probably have them for quite some time. These boots generally weigh three pounds or more.

BUYING BOOTS

The best time to go shopping for boots is in the afternoon or evening. Why? As we walk around during the day, our feet tend to swell, ending

Limmer heavyweight ("standard weight") hiking boot.

up larger than they were in the morning. Your feet are likely to swell even more after a day of carrying a pack. By shopping in the evening, you can avoid buying a boot that felt snug in the store, but feels like hell on earth after a day of hiking in the blazing sun.

Boot manufacturing is a profit-making business; hence hype and advertising gimmicks are involved. It is not the case that the fanciest high-tech name signifies the best boot. Most of what you see on first appearance will have nothing to do with the quality and fit of a boot. Keep this in mind. You are not out to buy something that will make you look good. You are out to buy a boot that will make everything golden for your feet and legs.

Before purchasing boots, examine them for manufacturing defects. Put the boot on a table and look at it from the back. The heel counter should sit vertical and the sole flat, without warping. Looking at the side, the toe area may turn up a little, giving a rocker effect, but this should not be too severe. Of course, every boot should be equal to its mate. Superficial scuffs, however, are of no significant importance.

Once you have a boot ready to try on, put on the socks you will likely use on upcoming hikes, and if you have orthotics, put them in the shoe. Put on both boots and lace them up. After you have laced a boot up, if the two sides of the upper touch, it is too wide; you won't be able to tighten your boots properly. Try a different style of boot. You should be able to wiggle your toes; however, the shoe should not be so big that the heel slips. Too tight a shoe will cause toe blisters, especially when walking downhill; and too loose a shoe will cause back-of-the-heel blisters, as the heel slips in the shoe. If possible, try walking downhill in boots before buying them. Have someone hold down the boot to the floor and see if you can raise your heel inside. If it slides up more than a fraction of an inch, it's too loose. Kick forward inside the boot. If your toes hit the tip, they are too tight. It is important that the boot be flexible enough to bend at the ball of the foot while holding the heel stable.

If your feet are of significantly different sizes, it is possible (but expensive) to buy mismatched boots. However, it is probably better to fit the boot to the larger foot and pad the boot for the smaller foot. To accommodate a slight limb length difference, you can add an extra insole to the short leg's boot. Using a full foot lift is preferable to only using a heel lift. If you need more than one-quarter inch, it is probably better to take the boot to a shoe repair store and have them add the appropriate lift to the outsole. If one foot is slightly smaller, the ideal way to pad the boot is to add a felt tongue pad, a one-quarter-inch piece of adhesive felt that is glued under the tongue of the boot. It keeps the foot pushed back in the shoe.

When buying boots, remember that they have three dimensions. People understand a shoe has length and width, but not everyone realizes that certain shoes have more depth in the toe box than others. This is the type of boot you should be looking for.

I personally do not see how it is possible to buy a shoe through mail order, unless you have tried on the exact boot in some store prior to ordering. Boots are so personal that they must be tried on. If you order by mail, be careful; be sure you can exchange the boots if necessary.

Once you have decided on a pair of boots, see if the store has a return policy. This policy enables you to wear the boots around the house and give them a shake-down to see if any potential problems creep up; step outside, however, and they're yours, whether they fit or not.

Breaking In Your Boots

Whether you buy a synthetic boot that's supple from the start, or a heavy-duty leather boot, **do not** take your new boot out on a long hike as soon as you walk out of the store; your feet will regret it and you may walk home in socks alone. Ideally, buy boots at least a month before you think you may use them on the trail. Even if the boots don't need to be broken in, your feet need to get used to the boot. Another warning: Do not buy a poor-fitting boot thinking it will get better once it's broken in. It's more likely that your boot will break in your feet. Boots must be comfortable from day one, maybe a little stiff but causing no pinching, no fifth toe irritation, no bunion pain, and no heel slippage.

The best way to break in boots is to wear them around the house. Put them on when you get home from work and wear them for a couple of hours. Work up to wearing them longer each day. When you're ready, take them for a short hike.

Boots need various amounts of breaking in. A heavy leather boot will require some conditioning and a long break-in period, perhaps 50 miles worth of short hikes. Some people speed up the break-in period by wetting their leather boots and wearing them until they dry out, but most manufacturers do not recommend this. It is also not suggested that you artificially heat the boot to break it in. Composite boots break in quicker than do leather boots.

One part of the boot that especially needs breaking in is the sole. It must be able to bend where your toes bend. If the sole is too stiff, it will affect your gait. You can take the boot in your hands and physically bend it to soften the sole, or you can try squatting with the boots on. The upper may also pinch your toes where the boot bends. You can help alleviate this by softening the upper with leather conditioners.

BOOT CARE

You've invested a lot of money in your boots. You want to make them last as long as you can. Before you even go out on the trail, you should waterproof and seal your boots. If your boots have a welt—a strip of material between the sole and upper to which both are sewn—use some sealer here. This will prevent water from leaking through the holes created by sewing, and it will protect the stitching. Waterproof and seal leather uppers, using NikWax, Biwell, Aquaseal, or SnowSeal products and reapply them periodically. If your boots have synthetic uppers, there isn't a lot you can do to increase their water repellence. If you have Goretex boots, you need to use a silicon-based treatment so as not to clog the pores in the fabric.

After you have returned from a hiking trip, make sure you clean your boots. Use a stiff brush to get off most of the dirt and dried mud, and with leather boots use a cleaner such as saddle soap. If the boots get wet (whether on the trail or at home), do not dry them by heating them—not by a fire, an oven, or hair dryer. They will shrink, crack, leak, and never be the same. Air-drying is best. You can also stuff boots with paper towels or newspaper to dry them inside. Check the laces and heels periodically and replace them when worn. It is normal to wear out the heel on the lateral (fifth toe) side. An overpronator will wear out the heel on the medial side. Obviously, walking on a warped heel will affect your gait. A good boot can be resoled. Remember that boots are an investment. Take care of them and they will take care of your feet.

ORTHOTICS

Many hikers have heard the term orthotics but have no idea what they are or how they relate to the feet. In general, an orthotic is an assistive device that helps a part of the body function properly. A foot orthotic alters the way the foot and leg move, enabling the bones and muscles to function in a way that is not painful or potentially harmful to the foot.

Not to be confused with sole inserts or heel cups available at drug stores, foot orthotics are custom made by a podiatrist and are based on the shape of an individual's foot. The first step in making an orthotic is to "capture" the shape of the individual's foot. There is technology available that allows a computer to scan feet, but the most common methods of capturing the unique shape of an individual's foot are taking an impression and making a mold. There are two basic techniques. The first uses a foam box, which the individual steps into, leaving an impression. There are some mail-order manufacturers that use this method. However, I do not recommend this technique because it captures the shape of the foot in its pathologic or "out-of-whack" position. The second technique uses a plaster cast to make a mold, which allows the podiatrist to position the foot into its proper biomechanical position. The orthotic made to fit such a cast will hold the foot in the appropriate position. A successful orthotic is only as good as the cast from which it is made.

A foot orthotic consists of: (a) a heel cup which grabs the heel to keep it as vertical as possible; (b) a heel post which controls the amount of STJ motion; (c) some arch support to limit flattening of the

Foot orthotic, top view.

arch; (d) a forefoot post to correct any angular deformity in the relationship of the forefoot to the rear of the foot; and (e) a top cover to
reduce friction and shearing forces, and to act as a shock absorber.

Depending on a patient's needs, foot orthotics can be made as
rigid as steel or as flexible as soft leather. You can't automatically con-
nect an orthotic type with a specific symptom. For example, heel pain
can occur in a flat foot and a high-arch foot for different reasons. The
proper orthotic type is chosen not for a symptom, but for a set of patient variables. The doctor must take into account the patient's age,
activity level, sports participation, and biomechanical problems. Remember, in general, flat feet need support and a more rigid orthotic,
while high-arch feet need more shock absorption and a softer orthotic.
The degree of rigidity, largely determined by the materials chosen, is
important to the success of the orthotic.

Orthotics are made from a variety of materials: thermoplastics, (this
often-used material is melted and molded onto the cast), polyethylene

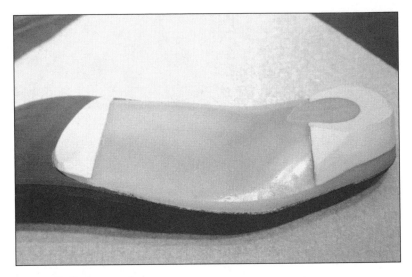

Foot orthotic, bottom view.

(this material is often used in conjunction with a computer scan of the foot, which is modified by a technician before the computer carves the orthotic from a solid block of polyethylene), graphite composites (this expensive, very thin material is a little rigid), or leather and cork (these are soft and thick but accommodating to the foot).

Not everyone needs custom orthotics, but if you do, consider getting the best insert you can. Your feet will thank you.

ARCH SUPPORTS AND SHOE INSERTS

Foot orthotics should not be confused with the arch supports, "cookies," and shoe inserts available over-the-counter (OTC) at many outdoor retail shops and drug stores. I won't go so far as to say not to try them. They are cheaper than orthotics, and if your problem is mild, they may help, but they are made in standard sizes to accommodate a standard size foot, with standard arch height, standard width, and standard rigidity—as if all feet were created equal! These products do

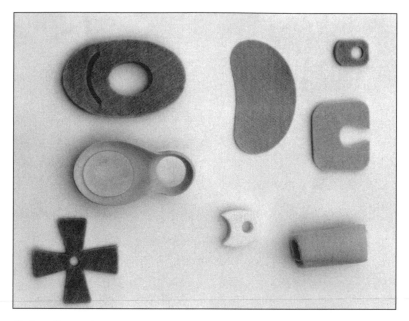

Various foot pads.

not control foot function like orthotics do; they pad the problem areas and ease symptoms, but they do not solve biomechanical problems.

Sof Sole and Sorbothane make a line of comfortable devices that run the gamut from soft foams, soft rubbers, and gels to hard plastic supports. Another manufacturer, Spenco, uses a neoprene similar to a diver's wet suit for its flat insoles. Neoprene has good cushioning and is great at preventing blisters. Some insoles have odor-absorbing characteristics, some have antifungal and antibacterial properties, and some absorb sweat well. However, those white "pillow" inserts with the tiny holes are almost useless. None of these inexpensive foam pads or arches has any significant effect.

You might consider this: if your doctor recommended eye glasses, would you go to your local drug store and try on glasses until one felt right, or would you go to an optometrist and be fitted for the exact lens you need? The same should be true of orthotics. Yes, there are some OTC inserts that you can try first, but if your problem persists, and you want to hike happy, then consider seeing a podiatrist for a custom-made orthotic.

OTHER EQUIPMENT

WATER FILTERS

You must bring enough liquid for your trip. I know it's heavy, but do not get caught short of water. Don't trust running streams' purity. They may look pristine, but alas, most streams and waterways are polluted either with chemicals or harmful microorganisms. There are siphon-type water purifiers and gravity-feed filters on the market. They filter out harmful microorganisms such as *E. coli, Giardia, Cryptosporidium,* and some harmful chemicals. When considering a filter, read the specs on the its ability to remove the different "livestock" found in water and determine if it has an "active" carbon filter to remove pesticides, heavy metals, and other chemicals. Water-purifying chemical tablets containing iodine are also available.

WALKING STICKS

How about a walking stick? You can either pick up a sturdy stick on the trail (one without rot, but don't take one that is alive either) or purchase a stylish accouterment to your outfit. It will give you another point of support, allow your arms to help uphill, and may just prevent a fall. It will also prove useful when crossing slippery streams and loose gravel. A good walking stick can maintain your walking rhythm, probe for marshy or muddy spots, and hold back prickly shrubs. It can even be used for protection against indigenous wildlife. Importantly, a walking stick reduces stress on the knees when going downhill. The quadriceps work overtime trying to prevent you from falling on your face. Every pound of pressure your arms absorb through the stick, when multiplied by thousands of steps, decreases enormously the stress on the knee joint.

There are attractive (but heavy) one-piece wood sticks or one, two, or three piece collapsible aluminum poles. These very lightweight and the collapsible ones pack well. They may even have an attachment for your camera, like a tripod, or a small storage space for money, matches, etc. The tip can be made of hard rubber or carbide. Both have pros and cons. Carbide is sturdy, heavy, noisy, and tough on the trail. Rubber is resilient and quieter but perhaps slippery when wet. In winter or on snow, a ski pole with basket works well. Most poles have a wrist strap. This is very useful in taking some of the pressure off your fingers and hand and transferring it to the wrists. The grips should be comfortable, with some ability to mold to your own grip. Some people prefer two poles, some only one. I prefer to keep one hand free. All poles should at least reach elbow height.

GAITERS

Gaiters are basically sleeves that go around your hiking boots. They are very useful in the winter to keep snow from slipping inside the boot. They do serve a purpose in warmer weather also. They keep stones, pebbles and dirt out of your boots—a most painful experience requiring you to stop, unlace, remove the offending boulder, and reboot. They consist of an outer layer made of various materials, a typically Velcro front closure, a top closure strap, instep strap, and another strap that goes under the sole of the boot to keep it from sliding up. They range from $30 to $300, depending on their quality. The most expensive are technical snow-boot gaiters. The upper material can either be canvas, nylon or Goretex. The lower material needs to be rip-resistant ballistic ripstop nylon, cordura, or a similar material. The top closure can either be a buckle or elastic strap; the front-closure Velcro should be one inch across and the "bootlace" a rugged strap with some type of buckle. Crocodiles, Rocky Mountain Gaiters, Black Diamond, and others manufacture a full line of different gaiters. The downside of gaiters is that they can be noisy, and they need to be breathable or your feet will overheat.

PACKS

One last point; when hiking, you will most likely have a pack on your back. You are never nimble with a pack, especially a heavy, 50-pound backpack. Even a lightweight day pack, with some food, water, and emergency supplies still has an effect on your gait. You lean forward to balance the weight on your back. Your shoulders mostly support these packs, whereas a larger backpack's weight is mostly supported by your hips. It is partly a pack's hip belt that allows your hips to bear the brunt of the weight. In this case, the weight is near your center of gravity, allowing a more upright walk. However, a heavy pack certainly saps your energy faster. Additionally, a backpack causes exaggerated overuse injuries, limits your stream-jumping ability, and upsets your stability. Short practice hikes are needed by any beginning backpacker. When purchasing a pack, do research and get the best you can afford. After all, your comfort is important, isn't it?

FIRST AID KITS

What makes a good emergency first aid kit? That depends on where you are hiking (any snakes, local environmental hazards?), when you are hiking (winter cold or summer heat?), how long you are going for (day trip versus extended trip), and how much you can realistically carry. The following is a suggested list. You should use your judgement, and add or subtract items you find are necessary to make the kit serve your needs.

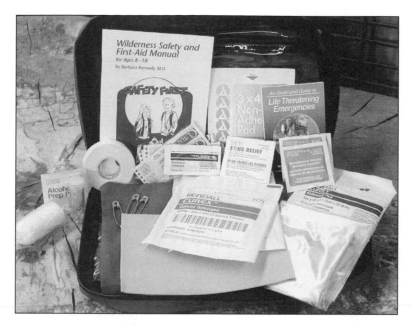

A typical backcountry first aid kit.

As you can see, there is no lack of ideas for an emergency kit's contents. You can build your own or purchase a kit from a sport company. Check out the web sites in the Appendix. But keep in mind that the best emergency kit in the world won't do you any good unless you know how to use the items in it. I highly recommend you take a first aid course, and if you spend a lot of time on the trail, a wilderness first aid course or some other intensive program will be invaluable to you— and others—should anything serious ever happen on the trail.

MAPS, COMPASSES, AND GPS UNITS

I know I feel naked when I go hiking without a trail map. I like to know where I am on the trail, what the next milestone is, when to switch trails, etc. If you are going into unfamiliar territory, I highly recommend getting a detailed map—the U.S. Geological Survey topographical maps

Suggested First Aid Kit

- #15 disposable scalpel
- Ace bandage
- alcohol wipes
- anaphylactic kit (if necessary)
- antibiotic ointment
- antiseptic towels
- Band-Aids
- bandage tape
- Betadyne wipes
- blister protection—moleskin, etc.
- burn cream (Silvadiene Rx)
- butterfly or Steri strip bandage
- cortisone cream
- CPR mask
- glucose (if diabetic)
- insect sting kit
- Kling wrap
- knife
- latex gloves
- oral antihistamine
- oral pain medication—Tylenol, ibuprofen, aspirin, etc.
- Sam splint
- Sawyer extractor
- scissors
- splinter forceps, tweezers
- sterile gauze squares
- stomach/nausea medicine
- sunburn cream
- sunscreen
- tick removal kit
- waterproof matches
- whistle or signal device
- any required prescription medications

provide the best overall detail for most areas in North America. A compass will also help you find your way, but neither a topographical map nor a compass will do you any good unless you know how to use them. Buy a book on the subject, or better yet, take a class in orienteering.

For us high-tech hikers, a handheld satellite global positioning system (GPS) can give you valuable information and some additional security in finding your way back. Though GPS units can be quite accurate and can be used to retrace your steps if need be, don't bet your safety on a piece of technology; be sure to include a compass in case the GPS unit breaks down.

Preparation and Maintenance

PRIMING THE HIKING ENGINE

Most people have had the experience of suddenly getting motivated to do some strenuous activity, then jumping into it with little preparation or warm-up. You pay the price later, when your back aches or some other seldom-used muscle complains at the injustice of not letting it know what was going to happen beforehand. Hiking is no different. Sure, you can throw on a pack and head for the hills, but without some preparation and forethought, you may end up a quivering mass a few hundred yards from the trailhead.

Even those of us who do stay in shape sometimes make the mistake of overextending ourselves—it's always easier to imagine hiking 20 miles in one day than actually accomplishing the trek. This is certainly not an admonition to stay home. Instead, it is wise, before you hike, to examine both the shape you are in and the coming challenges of hiking outdoors. This chapter aims to help keep your hiking engine running smoothly and efficiently.

The physical challenge of hiking requires certain components of fitness. One is cardiovascular fitness—healthy heart, lungs, and circulation. You must start out at a level your cardiovascular fitness will allow, and build up from there. The second component is muscle strength and endurance. Depending on the trail, some climbing strength may be required, and depending on the distance, your endurance will be tested.

The third component is flexibility: tight muscles injure easily. In the sections that follow, we'll examine each of these factors.

We'll also look at aspects of hiking that will help prevent injury: tips on taking care of your feet and legs, how to plan trips that don't overly tax your current physical ability, and some ideas on how to avoid accidents while on the trail itself.

FITNESS AND STAMINA

I hope you had not planned on going on a strenuous hike straight from your easy chair without some training. You probably maintain your hiking equipment, so why not your body? I know most hikers take great pains to keep their boots in top condition. Doing likewise with your body will have long-term benefits. Keeping fit in between your bouts of hiking is very important, especially as you age. Suddenly jumping into strenuous exercise can shock your system and cause overuse injuries. That's why keeping aerobically fit is important.

AEROBIC EXERCISE

Aerobic exercise by definition means "with oxygen." When you exercise at a certain level, your cardiovascular and respiratory system supplies oxygen to your muscles at a rate equal to their usage. That's why your pulse increases with activity; it's the heart's attempt to keep the blood flowing and maintain your cells' access to oxygen. When your muscles utilize oxygen faster than your circulation can supply it, you have begun what is called anaerobic exercise. When this occurs, lactic acid, a byproduct of anaerobic exercise, builds up in your muscles. The burning you feel in your leg muscles when you hike up a steep hill is a result of lactic acid buildup. When you rest and the oxygen level catches up to muscle usage, this lactic acid is metabolized in the normal aerobic pathways. In fact, you never exercise only aerobically or anaerobically. The amount that you exercise in one way or the other varies with different muscles, levels of exercise, and your fitness.

This is where training comes in. If you want to hike to those high mountain vistas, you need to work up to those strenuous hikes. Exercise strengthens heart muscle and improves heart efficiency, enabling your heart to make more oxygen available to muscles and delaying excessive anaerobic activity. It lowers your resting heart rate and increases the heart's ability to return to its resting rate faster. What are some other benefits to exercising aerobically? First, it improves cardiovascular fitness by increasing collateral circulation around clogged blood vessels and reducing the level of "bad cholesterol" (LDL and VLDL cholesterol) while increasing the "good cholesterol" (HDL).

How does aerobic exercise benefit hikers? As you improve your aerobic fitness, your ability to go up steep hills increases, and when you stop for a rest, you recover more quickly.

GETTING STARTED

Like any physical activity, it's best to start hiking at the level of activity you are currently familiar with, and slowly and gradually building up to more strenuous challenges. Let's return to the engine analogy. If your car is badly tuned, you can still get where you are going if you only drive a few miles per week; but try and push it, and you will certainly blow out a hose or some other important part, causing the car to come to a screeching halt. Likewise, if you are a sedentary type of person, a significant problem (cardiovascular or biomechanical) may go unnoticed while walking from your house to your car. But go on a 10-mile-long hike, and you might begin to wheeze and suffer, or even endanger your life. By beginning and continuing a weekly workout regime, you can start to work out the kinks in your own system.

If you have not had a physical in awhile, now's a good time to get one. Depending on your age, you may even want to test your cardiovascular fitness before you hit the trail. Check with your doctor.

Unless you are training for an Olympic event, it is not necessary to work out seven days a week, but you should attempt some type of exercise at least three times a week. This can be as simple as taking short walks early in the morning or after dinner. If you belong to a fitness club, work out there—you'll be less inclined to wimp out when inclement weather comes your way. These clubs have a broad range of aerobic equipment available, from stair climbers and stationary bikes to elliptical walkers and treadmills. I admit, you will probably not get the same level of aerobic activity on a machine as you will climbing even a modest mountain, but it is worth the effort to keep yourself in shape—especially if you live in an area with an "off season" (too cold, snowy, or hot).

While you are working out—either at your local gym or on the trail—you will want to use the chart below to help guide you in improving your aerobic ability. The chart refers to your target aerobic heart rate, based upon age. As you work out, you want your pulse to fall between the 60% and 80% rate. Below 60%, you really aren't improving a whole lot; above 80%, you may be taxing your heart too much. Be aware that your physician may suggest a different rate from that on the chart, depending on your medical history. As you exercise, the most important thing to remember is to work out at a rate that stresses your heart to between 60% and 80% of its estimated maximum heart rate for at least 20 sustained minutes. When you are training (and even when hiking), check your pulse by feeling on one side of your neck for your carotid pulse, or in your wrist, by your thumb between the tendons. Count your pulse for 15 seconds, then multiply by four. Speed up if you fall below 60%, slow down if you go above 80%.

Target Aerobic Heart Rate

Age	60% Max Heart Rate	80% Max Heart Rate
20	120	160
25	117	156
30	114	152
35	111	148
40	108	144
45	105	140
50	102	136
55	99	132
60	96	128
65	93	124
70	90	120
75	87	116
80	84	112

Information from American Academy of Sports Medicine.

A very general way of estimating your maximum heart rate is to subtract your age from 220. Then multiply it by either 0.8 or 0.6 to get the 80% or 60% maximum heart rate for your age.

Over time, you will hit a plateau and your progress will be thwarted; this is your body's attempt to catch up with itself. Don't get frustrated. Continue to work out and more improvement will come. Ideally, you should exercise every other day, increasing mileage slowly; a weight lifting regime on alternate days is a good way to balance out things (as well as increase your strength).

Of course, you did stretch before starting your workout and after cooling down, didn't you? In training, you should never schedule two "heavy" days of exercise in a row. And during your workout, alternate light and heavy (or different) exercises. Over the course of several weeks or months, you might try switching your routines around. Switch from walking to bicycling to swimming as is reasonable.

Keep in mind that you can injure yourself even off the trail. Injury to the legs is typically due to overuse. Muscles unaccustomed to work will start to complain. Using common sense, it is important to build up to a certain level slowly, pushing yourself just a little more each time. There is some truth in the phrase "no pain, no gain," but please, don't overdo it.

DIETING

Working out is not the only way to keep in shape. Eating well-balanced meals is just as important. You might ask, "what's the best diet plan to use?" Why do you think there are so many dieting fads? The fact is, if one worked, there would be only one on the market! How could low-fat, high-fat, no-protein, high-protein, low-carbohydrate, high-carbohydrate, no-carbohydrate, high-water, and synthetic-shake diets all be successful? The most detrimental aspect of dieting is the potential guilt associated with falling off the wagon. The guilt over one cookie can be tremendous (usually causing the ingestion of another nine cookies topped off with a scoop of ice cream).

If you try to micromanage your caloric intake, it can get damn depressing. The point is that even a 20-minute hike can help reduce weight by increasing the calories your body burns—without starving. So enjoy one cookie a day and walk. This way, you can turn guilt, depression, and anxiety about your weight into an uplifting, head-clearing

Calorie-Burning Activities

Average calories burned per 60 minutes in a 150 lb. person:

- golf   250
- karate   350
- bicycling fast   500
- hiking (3 mph)   450
- cross-country
  skiing (4 mph)   600

- dance   340
- tennis   420
- swimming slowly   450
- jogging (5 mph)   750

On average it will take 67 minutes to work off a hamburger, 19 minutes to work off an apple, 10 minutes for your average cookie, 20 minutes for a sugary soda, and 13 minutes for an orange.

---

aerobic activity. If you are diabetic, however, it **is** important to micro-manage your caloric intake and your oral medications, as well as to time your insulin injections so as to keep your blood glucose level as close to normal as possible.

Even if you aren't diabetic, this is not to say you should eat whatever, whenever, and however much you want. Just as when you put bad gas in your car and its performance suffers, the same can be said for our bodies if we dine continually on high-fat junk food. The main things to keep in mind when dieting are eating healthy foods, exercising, and when you do eat "bad" food, do so in moderation.

Hiking is an excellent way of achieving good cardiovascular fitness and reduced weight. The only way to effectively lose weight is to increase calories burned and decrease calories eaten. Starving is not a successful way to lose weight.

Stretching and Strengthening Exercises

From a pro-prevention point of view, all hikers need to stretch their hamstrings and calf muscles to avoid injury. Anyone who exercises regularly tends to strengthen the muscles in the back of the leg (hamstrings and calf muscle) more than those in the front of the leg (the quadriceps and anterior tibial). Because of this imbalance, the hamstrings and calf muscles tend to get tight, causing potential problems with the foot, ankle, knee, and back. A tight muscle does not have the flexibility to quickly adapt to irregular terrain or an unbalanced step and is more apt to tear under stress (like when jumping a stream with a 40-pound backpack). That's why stretching is always a good idea. There are also exercises that will strengthen the front leg muscles, helping to offset this imbalance.

Below are several stretching exercises that help the hiker prevent injury. In general, all exercises should be performed for five seconds, and repeated five times. **Never** bounce when stretching; hold the stretching stance to the point of pain, not past it. Any significant pain felt while stretching should be evaluated by a physician or podiatrist. There are many different stretches—some are standard and some are more creative. Find the ones that work for you and stick with them. Avoid ones in which you don't have complete control over the stretch. You know the stretch where you drape a leg over a fence and try to touch your toe? I don't like the idea of having your entire body weight against your weakest joint—your knee—so a little slip could tear up your knee instead of stretching it. Be careful of toe touches if you have a back problem. A physiatrist, physical therapist, or trainer can help provide specific exercises for individual needs or in response to specific injuries, but I will describe my favorites.

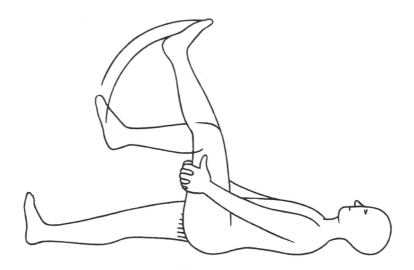

Stretching exercise # 1: hamstrings.

First, note that exercises attempting to strengthen the foot muscles to support the arch are a complete and total waste of time—the foot just doesn't work that way. We can rid the world, here and now, of the myth of picking up marbles with your toes to strengthen the arch (and other such nonsense).

It is, however, a good habit to stretch and warm up all your muscles before starting a hike, and stretch again when finished. Keep in mind that these are preventative exercises.

HAMSTRINGS

EXERCISE #1

This exercise helps loosen up your hamstrings. Do the following:

Lay on your back, keeping one leg flat.

Raise your other leg so your thigh is straight up—perpendicular to the floor—but keep your knee relaxed.

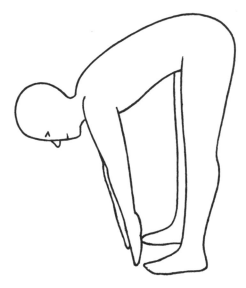

Stretching exercise # 2: hamstrings.

Pull your lower leg up by straightening your knee. Do not let your thigh drop or pull it up past perpendicular.

Pull as hard as you can without causing pain until your leg is as straight up as you can get it. If it is within 5–10° of straight, you're ok. If the angle your lower leg makes with your thigh is more like 30–45°, then you are like me—in need of some heavy duty stretching.

Stretch for five seconds; repeat five times.

Switch legs.

EXERCISE #2

If your back is OK, you can do this toe-touching exercise. If you can touch your toes, great; but if you can't, don't worry—you may never be able to. Your goal is to cut the distance from fingers to floor in half. NEVER BOUNCE. Do the following:

Separate your legs by about 12 inches.

Stretching exercise # 3: calf.

Keep your knees locked.

Attempt to touch your right little toe.

Attempt to touch between your feet.

Attempt to touch your left little toe.

Holding each pose five seconds; repeat five times.

CALF

EXERCISE #3

My favorite calf-stretching exercise is familiar to most; however, there are right and wrong ways to do it. First, find a wall and do the following:

Face the wall, one foot in front of the other, about 18 inches away.

This is important—slightly turn your toes inward on both feet (like pigeon toes).

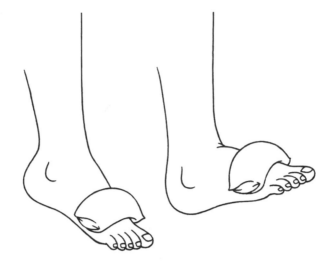

Stretching exercise # 4: anterior tibial.

Keep your back knee locked and your heel flat on the ground.

Bend your front knee and lean in towards the wall. Keep your head up.

You should feel a very strong pulling behind your back knee. If not, check your position or move slightly further away from the wall. **Don't bounce.**

Hold five seconds; repeat five times.

Switch legs.

There are also night splints and other devices, such as Pro Stretch®, available to help stretch your calf muscle.

Anterior Tibial

EXERCISE #4

Those prone to shin splints or pain in the front of the lower leg need to do strengthening exercises. Either make a 1–2-pound sand bag or buy a donut-type weight and apply it to the top of your foot across the instep, then do the following:

Sit so your foot is dangling.

Pull your foot up as high as you can (dorsiflex it)—only your foot, not your leg.

Hold for five seconds; repeat five times.

Switch feet.

Increase weights slowly.

QUADRICEPS

EXERCISE #5

This strengthening exercise is excellent for those with chronic knee pain, especially around the kneecap, but it takes some help.

The key to this exercise is that the knee never moves. The reason is that you don't want to grind your kneecap into the femur with added weight. You only want to strengthen the muscle.

You may want to use an OTC or physician-dispensed knee brace. One such device is made out of neoprene (like a diver's wet suit) with a hole for the kneecap and extra support to keep it tracking in its groove.

You will need to buy or make one- to five-pound weights, similar to those described in Exercise #4.

Sit with your knee extended straight out in front of you.

Have someone place the weight across your ankle and hold for five seconds.

Remove the weight **without moving the knee** for five seconds.

Replace the weight, repeating five times.

Switch legs.

Slowly increase the weight.

The importance of stretching back muscles before a hike cannot be overemphasized. Increasing your flexibility, balance, extensibility, and stability can only create a more rewarding experience.

There are a great many stretching exercises for the back. The following are some basic stretches that can be of value to the general hiker. These do not encompass the entire range of rehabilitative exercises. People with back or neck problems should not attempt these exercises without getting specific recommendations from a physician or chiropractor. Any exercise that causes pain should be discontinued and discussed with your health care provider.

Standing back stretch

Stand erect, and place your hands on your buttocks, fingers pointing down. Bend backwards to produce a gentle stretch. Hold for 5 to 10 seconds. Repeat 10 times or as tolerated.

Torso side bends

Stand erect, then bend your torso sideways from the waist until you feel a gentle stretch. Hold for 5 to 10 seconds. Repeat 3 sets of 10 or as tolerated.

Torso twist

Stand erect, arms extended from the sides (forming the letter T). Slowly rotate the torso sideways in one direction to produce a gentle stretch. Hold 5–10 seconds and rotate in the other direction. Repeat three sets of 10 or as tolerated.

Pelvic tilt

Lie on your back, knees bent, and rock your pelvis by arching your back as far as possible. Hold 5 to 10 seconds, then rock your pelvis in the

opposite direction by flattening your lower back against the floor. Hold
5 to 10 seconds. Repeat 3 sets of 10 or as tolerated.

Knees to forehead

Like the pelvic tilt, lie on your back, knees bent. Pull one or both knees
up towards your head, while simultaneously pulling your head to your
knees. Hold 5 to 10 seconds. Repeat 10 times or as tolerated.

Donkey kick

Assume a crawl position, hands and knees on the floor. Extend one leg
up and back while raising the contralateral arm (e.g., left leg and right
arm). Hold 5 to 10 seconds. Repeat each side 10 times or as tolerated.

Torso Stretch

Assume a crawl position as in the donkey kick and gently lower fore-
head to the floor with the arms extended in front of you. Hold 5 to 10
seconds. Repeat 10 times or as tolerated.

FOOT PREPARATION

Getting and remaining in shape and making sure you stretch before
physical exercise is only part of the battle. If you do not take care of
your feet, all the aerobic ability in the world won't help you avoid pain.

Long nails in a hiking boot can increase the chances of a "black
nail," or a blood blister under the nail. They can also cut into the adjacent toe and cause a bleeding mess. Imagine walking miles with one
nail acting like a knife blade, cutting into another toe. So the first
thing you want to do is trim your toenails. Whether you use scissors or
clippers doesn't matter. A knife is definitely not recommended—not
only might you slip and slice your toes, knives also leave a ragged edge
that can end up being very painful. Trim the toenails short and

straight across. This reduces the chance of ingrown toenails. Do not clip out the corners. Use a nail file to smooth any rough edges.

Now look over your foot, your heel, and any other places that may have given you trouble in the past. Mild, painless calluses need not be treated—they are the skin's response to excessive pressure. However, if you have painful corns or calluses, they should be attended to by a podiatrist before you go out on your hike. Please note: I **strongly advise** that you **do not** use OTC corn remedies. They are all salicylic acid preparations that cause an acid burn. You don't need a corn **and** an acid burn on your toe before a hike! See the First Aid chapter for further discussion on corns and calluses.

If you know the areas you have had problems with blisters in the past, you may want to intervene and protect those areas before you even start hiking. Typical blister-prone areas include the back of the heel, the toes, and the ball of the foot. Use either moleskin, Spenco Second Skin, Spyroflex Skin Saver, a Dr. Scholl's product, or other blister-prevention coverings for bony prominences you know from past experience are likely to blister. Plastic Band-Aids are not recommended on the feet—which are too sweaty—nor is duct tape a good solution, except in a pinch.

Finally, consider whether you have a sweating problem. Everyone has his or her own "thermostat" to trigger sweating. Some sweat profusely. The medical term is bromhydrosis. Besides being embarrassing, it causes uncomfortable foot problems. The excess in moisture increases the friction on your feet and toes, making it more likely you will get blisters. If blisters are a common problem, you might try an OTC powder—either cornstarch or talc, with or without antifungal medication—or the use of sock liners and more breathable boots. A tea soak may even help (tannic acid is a drying agent).

For excessive sweating, you can use an OTC antiperspirant made for the feet such as bromilotion; or a prescription medication like Drysol;

or Xerac, an aluminum chloride and alcohol preparation. I recommend you stay away from formaldehyde preparations unless all else fails. Some people recommend Vaseline around "hot spots." Some swear by it, some think it grossly uncomfortable. In any event, keep it away from the area between the toes.

PLANNING YOUR HIKE

The prevention of many injuries begins with the planning of your trip. The most common mistake hikers make is overestimating their ability. Rested and in the comfort of home, it's easy to fool oneself into believing that a 3-day, 60-mile trip is easily attainable. Once on the trail, the reality is eye-opening.

Whether you are planning a trip on your own or with a hiking club, here are some factors you should consider before going too far into the planning process.

LENGTH — How far you can walk each day depends largely upon your stamina and strength. How fit are you? What's the longest hike you have ever been on? What's the longest hiking day you've ever experienced? The longer you walk, the more you get tired, and the greater your chance of injury due to misjudgment. Before you head off down the trail, be honest about the distance you can reasonably hike before you resemble the walking dead.

Once on the trail, taking occasional breaks will greatly extend your overall daily mileage. For those who go on long-distance hikes, stamina increases; after several weeks of hiking, you're less likely to get as tired doing the same mileage that exhausted you when you first started out. The key is to not overextend yourself those first few weeks.

ELEVATION — Elevation can affect the hiker, especially flatlanders, in two ways. The most evident is the reduced amount of oxygen available at higher elevations. Depending on what shape you are in, elevations as little as 5,000 or 6,000 feet can leave you sucking wind as you climb that steep trail. Whether you're effected at 6,000 or 12,000 feet, reduced oxygen capacity means reduced faculties—so your chance of making bad judgements increases.

If you are going to hike in higher elevations, be sure to either allow several days of acclimatization before you hike (near or at the altitude at which you will be hiking), or if you can't wait, scale back the miles and elevation you plan on covering in the first few days until you do get acclimatized. It is also smart to heed this bit of backcountry advice: hike high, sleep low.

The other concern for high-altitude hikers is the sun. Since the atmosphere isn't as thick in the mountains as it is at sea level, you can quickly get dehydrated and sunburned; both hamper your ability to make clear decisions. Drink lots of liquid and use plenty of sunscreen and lip balm to prevent these problems.

Another more serious problem not directly associated with the feet and legs can also develop at high altitudes (8,000 feet and higher). Acute mountain sickness (AMS) can effect people for various reasons, including ascending too high too fast. Symptoms for mild cases of AMS include nausea, headache, irritability, confusion, and altered sleep. More serious cases (usually occurring above 13,000 feet) include severe headache, listlessness, vomiting, and coma. Though in many cases losing elevation helps, it is best to check a competent first aid book (see Appendix) for prevention and treatment.

DESERT — In the desert and other arid regions, you may not feel thirsty until it's too late. Becoming dehydrated tires you out, again increasing the chance of injury. It is not uncommon for the body to require four or more liters of water in a full day of hiking. On my summer dinosaur digs, the conditions are often 100°F and zero humidity. I will take a frozen one-liter bottle of water and at least two other liters of water with me. I add water to the frozen bottle as needed. It is more than a treat to have cold water on a hot trail—but be careful, drinking too much may give you cramps. If you hike in these environments, plan to hike during early mornings, late afternoons, and evenings to reduce exposure to the sun, and rest in shaded areas during the heat of the day. Also take into account the need to carry extra water (and the additional weight that entails).

TERRAIN — This can play an important part in determining your energy level. Obviously, rocky, uneven trails make you exert more energy and tire you out more quickly than do flat trails. Also be aware of the elevation gain along a trail. Level hikes are easier, while multiple up and down segments can exert their toll—going up a hill is hard, but coming down the other side is brutal on knees. Plan on shorter hikes if you are hiking in a particularly hilly area or at least plan to take more frequent and longer-lasting breaks.

FOOD AND WATER — These are not just a concern in extreme environments. Becoming dehydrated is a sure way to impair your judgement. Always carry enough water with you, and be prepared in case expected water sources are dry.

As with water, skimp on food and you may find your energy failing late in the day. This will also impair your judgement, possibly leading to missteps or poor decisions. Replenish those burned calories. Make sure your carry enough food and snacks to sustain you throughout the trip. A good source of energy along the trail is "gorp." This traditional hiker's food is mostly dried fruits, nuts, sunflower seeds, raisins, and carob. It is high in energy (yes, calories) and easy to carry. You can make your own or buy a prepackaged mix. That and a juice box may be all you need for a short afternoon hike. But do plan in advance for your nutritional needs.

S E A S O N S — Depending on where you live, you probably experience extremes in one season or another, whether it be winter or summer. Cold and hot extremes have specific concerns that you need to consider before venturing out. See more on this under Environmental Risks below.

W E A T H E R — If you are going on a weekend trip, check the forecast for the time you will be out. If the forecast calls for inclement weather and you are particularly cautious, you can delay your hike. However, keep in mind that even the best weather forecasters can be wrong; unexpected showers can dampen the most cautious among us. If it does rain, your footing will be more suspect. Take your time and make sure to place your feet on secure sections of trail. Unless you have experience in cold weather hiking, you might want to consider delaying your trip if the forecast calls for snow or ice. Be aware that the hot summer weather at the base of a mountain can turn into a snowstorm at the summit. Just ask anyone who has climbed Mount Washington in New Hampshire. Be prepared for the weather.

Long-distance hikers may want to carry a radio to keep abreast of changing weather. You may not be able to avoid what's coming, but you can at least be prepared—cutting the day's hike short to take advantage of a nearby cabin or shelter.

When planning a hike, most people probably choose an area they want to hike in, then select the trail they intend to follow. Experience certainly helps, but know your limits. If you are relatively inexperienced, err on the conservative side and start off with easier hikes— short ones that cover fairly easy terrain—then go for more challenging ones later, after you have tested yourself. If you are going with a hiking club or some other group, talk with the group leader about the difficulty of the hike and whether it is right for your abilities. Once you have gone on several trips, you will get a better feel for your limits.

Part of your preparation should involve some research. Know your route and what to expect. Read a map, ask a friend, read a trail guide, ask a local resident, or surf the Internet. Know the round-trip distance. Can you do that distance or will you end up sore tomorrow, with shin splints or swollen knees? Will the trail be paved, gravel, dirt, mud, or rocky? Will you have to cross any streams or scramble over rocks?

If you are gung-ho and decide to try a more challenging hike, keep in mind that it helps to be flexible. If you find that you have bitten off more than you can chew, make alternate plans. Good planning involves contingency plans should someone get sick or hurt; knowing where along the trail you can bail from a hike is as important as any other aspect of the planning process. If cutting the hike short isn't possible, take an extra day or two to spread out the miles a little thinner.

ON THE TRAIL

You've made your plans, bought the food, loaded the pack, and now you are at the trailhead where all your planing and preparation will be put to the test. Still, there are some things you need to consider while hiking so that you can continue to have a safe trip.

HIKING TECHNIQUES

While hiking can be a walk through Central Park or Golden Gate Park (depending on your coast), often you will not have perfectly-groomed trails. There are streams, rocks, roots, holes, loose gravel, rutted trails,

Eyes on the Trail

I recently went to eastern Montana on a dinosaur expedition. The "badlands" of Montana are filled with coulees and mudstone, with occasional sinkholes that seem to go to China. It is an area of exposed Cretaceous rock, dating back 65 million years—to the very end of the dinosaurs. My friend found the jaw of a hadrosaur (a duckbill dinosaur).

After digging it out and jacketing it with plaster, it must have weighed 30 pounds. Guess how it was removed from the field? Human power—not even a four-wheel drive could make it out there. Walking with a heavy, irregular weight was difficult and

tiring, even with help. Well, after one mile, he was tired and not looking where he was going. He took a step into a small sinkhole and started to tumble. Luckily, his personal damage was minimal, and with very acrobatic juggling, the dinosaur fossil was unharmed. This is a good example of how exhaustion can create a potentially serious problem from a slight misstep.

It is also a good example of the value of knowing where your second step is going to be, before you make your first step. If your first step is not as stable as you had thought, you can shift quickly to the next step.

washed-out and eroded areas, etc. This is where flexibility is important. Tight muscles cannot respond to a slight twist or slip; they will tear. Flexible muscles will compensate for a sudden unexpected motion by stretching that extra bit. Accidents happen, especially on rocks and in streams; some care can prevent many mishaps.

Streams

To avoid injury on the trail, keep in mind that stream crossings deserve particular attention. You may want to look a bit up and down the trail for a handy bridge of rocks in the streambed (remember that rocks will be slippery). Don't be a circus high-wire performer and take an elevated log standing up—sit or crawl across it. Before you consider stepping into the stream, consider the depth and speed of the water. If you've ever canoed, you know how much force moving water can exert. A fast-moving stream can easily knock you off your feet. Don't go across barefoot; crossing barefoot is a great way to puncture, abrade, contuse, or sprain a foot or ankle. Hikers who expect to encounter streams will often carry a spare lightweight pair of tennis shoes to cross with. Of course, you can keep your boots on and "ford the stream" (in warm weather only). This is a place where a walking stick can definitely help. As you walk across, make sure you know where your feet are going and if the traction is acceptable. Keep one foot firmly planted as you explore for your next step, and only shift your weight to the next step if you know it is secure.

Rock Scrambling

There is nothing like the added excitement and challenge of climbing past a stretch of loose rocks, boulders, and mountain outcrops. Remember: if it's tough to climb up, climbing down will be even trickier. Use your hands for extra points of support, and make each footstep count. Try to have three points of contact—two feet and a hand, or both hands and one foot. Test each step carefully, with a hand-grip if possible. Know that if one foot slides back, the other is still firmly planted. Anticipate a slide, and know where you might end up.

Also be mindful of those climbing above you. Follow too close behind and you won't have time to react to falling rocks. If you have people following you, make sure you warn them of rocks you dislodge by yelling, "Watch out!" or "Rock!"

Walking on mudstone is a challenge in itself. When wet, it is slippery; when dry, it is slippery and sharp. Going uphill, you need to choose your steps carefully, taking advantage of any rock or foothold and remembering this rule: know where your second step will be before making your first. Going downhill on mudstone, however, is more like skiing—also called "sole surfing." This is difficult to control and potentially dangerous. There occasionally comes a time in a hike when walking will no longer do. That's when I like to use the seated position, also called "tush trimming." Lowering your center of gravity by placing four limbs and one tush on the ground provides you greater control.

Hiking Uphill

Gravity is relentless. Even a small grade can sap your strength after a few miles. In fact, it is amazing how a small stretch of level ground can restore your energy. This is obviously where good cardiovascular fitness comes in. If you are looking to improve your fitness, a hike with multiple up-and-downhill segments may be just for you. Consider using your walking stick so your upper body can help you, and take frequent breaks.

Hiking Downhill

You would think that going downhill should be a breeze, but once again gravity is a problem. Imagine a truck at the top of a mountain just starting downhill in neutral—with no brakes! Obviously, it will continue to pick up speed, eventually going out of control until something stops it. Well, your brakes are your leg muscles, the ones in front—and your knees and ankles are the areas of maximum impact. Basically, when hiking downhill, you are exerting force to keep yourself from falling out of control. Your front leg muscles (quadriceps and anterior tibial muscles) take quite a beating. Your lower legs shake from fatigue, your knees swell, your steps become unstable, and injuries occur. In fact, more problems occur when walking downhill than uphill.

It is a constant battle for control. My advice is the same as for uphill: know your limitations and build up slowly.

ENVIRONMENTAL RISKS

Both winter and summer create conditions hikers need to be aware of, health-wise.

Winter brings its own beauty and rewards. The trails are empty; the air is crisp, clean, and cold, and the white snow pristine. However, nothing works as smoothly in winter—especially fingers, but feet and legs, too. Sweating should be of particular concern for hikers. Sweating and then freezing is unhealthy.

In winter, layering clothing becomes very important. You must wear enough clothes to maintain body temperature, but as you hike you will warm up and sweat. This isn't a problem as long as you are moving, exerting energy, and creating body heat. But take a break, and you can quickly get chilled. Don't hesitate to start shedding clothes as you warm up. Also, make sure you wear breathable layers and clothes next to the skin that have wicking capabilities. Consider changing your socks if they get damp. Ideally, winter boots should be extra water-resistant. Overboots are available which provide an extra waterproof and insulating layer over your boots. There are also boots made of rubber specifically for wet and snowy weather.

Don't forget dark sunglasses, hat, and gloves—sunlight reflects brightly from snow, but your extremities are still vulnerable to the cold air. Don't plan on going too fast in snow. You can bring a thermos of hot soup for the trail. Lastly, if applicable, obtain information concerning avalanche risk and storm warnings from the park's ranger. Winter weather can turn bad quickly—be prepared and give your location to the ranger or friends at home.

Some common, cold-weather hiking injuries include chilblains, trench foot, and immersion foot. These are caused by cold, damp conditions; freezing temperatures are not needed for them to occur. Tingling, redness, and blisters may appear; also, the skin may look wrinkled (pruned). Treatment consists of first drying out and warming up the foot, and then applying emollient creams. More severe, frostbite occurs from extreme exposure to cold and necessitates professional care.

At the other extreme are heat and related heat-stress injuries, more common to summer hiking. As you know, the body regulates excess heat by perspiration and evaporation. This sweating can lead to dehydration, which is the big risk in heat injuries. Prevention consists of slow acclimatization, proper sun-shielding clothing, a hat, and adequate fluid and electrolyte (salt) intake. Certain prescription medications can increase your risk of dehydration.

The calf muscles and stomach are prone to heat cramps. These may be associated with general heat disorders including extreme thirst (not a surprise), nausea, dizziness, and rapid pulse. Treatment is obvious: slowly drink large volumes of water with electrolytes. Salt tablets should be used only in extreme circumstances and must be accompanied by a large amount of fluid. Do not take salt tablets without proper liquids. Salted foods or drinks are preferred. Heat cramps and heat exhaustion are relatively common conditions and easily cared for with common sense. Heat stroke, however, is a medical emergency. It is a complete breakdown of the body's cooling system. Sweating ceases and core body temperature rises to extreme levels (115°F). Emergency treatment includes wet compresses and ice, if available, to immediately reduce body temperature, followed by hospitalization. For further information, consult medical texts or your doctor.

First Aid

R E P A I R I N G   T H E   H I K I N G   E N G I N E

Walking is so natural that we seldom think about the consequences of foot or leg injuries until we suddenly experience them. Who hasn't misstepped on a particularly rooty section of trail or tweaked their ankle on a steep stair or switchback? Hopefully the pain was momentary and you were able to continue. But what would you do if you had a serious injury far from the trailhead? Even something as simple as a blister, if left unattended, can quickly debilitate a hiker with excruciating pain.

Trouble in the outdoors appears in one of two ways: fast and furious, or slow and insidious. A fall, a cut, or an insect or animal bite can come out of nowhere. A momentary lapse in judgment or just plain dumb luck can leave you injured. There is only so much you can do to prevent these injuries, but you can keep aware of changing environmental conditions (in both weather and terrain) as well as your own changing condition: is cold, hunger, thirst, or fatigue hindering your coordination or judgement? Have you overstepped your abilities? Catch trouble early, when it is small and easily handled.

Slow and insidious injuries are much more preventable. Usually a hiker's body offers warning signs that say it's time to slow down, take a break, or seek treatment. If these signs are ignored in order to reach a mileage goal or site, the result can be very painful. I learned this early in my hiking career.

In my preprofessional youth, I was quite the adventurous hiker. Once, after "studying our brains out," my friends and I took a hike up Mount Tamalpias (Mount Tam) outside of San Francisco—a most beautiful area with majestic redwoods. There was fog swirling in the valleys and perfect blue skies above. I donned powder and cotton tube socks. I had worn my boots before, but never up a mountain. They had occasionally irritated the back of my heel, but I thought "no big deal." Mount Tam's elevation is not severe, but it seems every step is straight up. The scenery was spectacular; my old manual Canon 35mm camera was spewing out slides by the dozen, just waiting for Kodak to perform its magic on them. After 90 minutes, I barely noticed a slight burning in the back of my heels, just past the threshold of sensation. However, the views were so overwhelming that I determined pain was not an option.

After 30 more minutes, my heels were definitely starting to talk to me; they were saying, "Do something now before it's too late!" Removing my boots, I saw a patch of cherry-red skin developing on the back of each heel, and all I had were Band-Aids. I put two on each heel, straightened my sweaty socks, rebooted, and was off—thinking I was so clever. Within 15 minutes, the Band-Aids started to shift and the plastic's friction against my skin worsened the burning. Suddenly, pain was definitely an option. The beautiful scenery was barely noticeable and every step was torture. How fast things change! A beautiful hike became an exercise in stamina.

When we finally reached the summit, I had blisters the size of half-dollars on my heels. Luckily for me, a septuagenarian came to my rescue. He punctured the blister, put on mercurochrome (it was a long time ago, and, yes, it did burn like hell), some gauze, and moleskin. I made it down the mountain in relative comfort and had a boot burning party that weekend. Sound familiar?

This chapter examines most of the injuries and problems you're likely to encounter while hiking. The first part looks at injuries that aren't area-specific—they could occur on your arms or torso as well as your feet and legs. The second part looks at problems specific to the feet or legs.

One final concern: when does an injury or problem necessitate leaving the trail? This is often a matter of personal decision, depending upon an individual's threshold of pain or the seriousness of the injury, though in cases of serious trauma the decision to leave the trail is a no-brainer. For short trips, toughing it out is certainly an option; while on long-distance hikes, taking several days off can do a world of good and prevent problems that follow you after you have finished.

GENERAL INJURIES

SKIN INJURIES

Burns

I am hard-pressed to imagine burning a foot or leg while hiking, but it could happen, especially among firewalkers. Camping with a roaring fire could definitely cause accidental burns, and being clumsy around a gas stove could lead to injury.

Should you be unlucky enough to burn yourself, here are some important do's and don'ts about burns. First, obviously remove the victim from further injury, extinguish any flames by rolling the person, blanketing him or her, or dousing the flames with water. Cool the area as best as possible, remove burned clothing that is **not** sticking to the skin. Check the ABC's of first aid—airway, breathing, and circulation.

TREATMENT: First-degree burns are red and painful but not swollen. On the trail, they are best treated by cool compresses, Silvadiene cream, and a fluffy dressing. Second-degree burns are very painful, with blistering and swelling. They are treated similarly but require the attention of a physician, possibly also narcotic pain killers, oral antibiotics, and physical therapy to help prevent scarring. Third-degree burns encompass the entire skin layer—possibly the muscle and bone below—and must be treated at a special burn center. The best thing you can do for badly-burned individuals is to safely remove them from further injury and make them as comfortable as possible until help arrives.

You may be able to continue hiking with a first-degree burn, depending on the area burned and how painful it is. You should treat second- and third-degree burns very seriously—the victim should be carried out and should not attempt to walk.

Cuts

Cuts come in many shapes, forms, and sizes, and can occur on most parts of the body, particularly the exposed areas, like arms and legs (that's why I tend to wear long pants, and when the weather suits, long-sleeve shirts). It is better to tear your pants if you slip and fall than to tear your skin. Pants do not experience pain, but skin does. And though I admonish you to always wear something on your feet to protect them from cuts and scrapes, inevitably there will be times when you must cross a stream and you don't have a spare set of shoes, or you need something just out of reach, but you don't want to put your stinky boots back on just to get it.

TREATMENT: The most common cuts you'll experience are the scrapes and abrasions one encounters while walking through brush or stepping accidentally into a blackberry bush. These injuries should be allowed to bleed. Then, using water and gauze, they should be cleansed. Flush them with as much clean water as possible and remove any dirt (do not use stream water, because it can introduce nasty microorganisms). Ideally, you can then whip out your Betadyne-soaked towellete, some antibiotic ointment, and the appropriate-sized bandage. A handkerchief and water will work in a pinch. Deeper cuts are treated the same way, but thorough cleansing is more important. You don't want to trap any dirt or bacteria in a deep wound. A Steri-Strip or butterfly wound closure can then be used to keep the wound closed until you are safely home.

For serious lacerations, direct pressure is the best way to staunch the flow of blood. It may appear that the bleeding will never stop, but it always does. Just be calm and patient. Also, remember that a little bit of blood looks like a lot of blood—especially if it is yours. If possible, immobilize the lacerated area. If it's on the bottom of the foot, keep the foot from bearing weight. Construct a "crutch" from a branch and use a buddy for support. Aspirin inhibits platelets and will worsen bleeding, so avoid its use. Tylenol does not affect bleeding.

Puncture wounds are a little different. They have the greatest potential for infection. For instance, a nail that punctures through a boot into the foot may carry dirt and shoe debris deep into the wound. These can fester into a nightmare of an infection. My advice for most puncture wounds is to seek medical care upon return for possible X-rays, exploration of the puncture, antibiotics, etc. While on the trail, try to flush the wound with water, apply Betadyne and antibiotic ointment, and cover the wound. Keep the wounded area from bearing weight if possible.

A foreign body—a splinter, for example—can be a nuisance on the trail. If it isn't bothering you, leave it until you get home. Depending on the extent of the injury, trail surgery will require the use of your splinter forceps, scalpel or knife, Betadyne, antibiotic ointment, and bandage. "Operating" on the bottom of your own foot is quite a challenge, but it can be done.

In most cases, you should be able to continue hiking. If you are on an extended hike, keep an eye on any cuts or scrapes to make sure they don't get infected and lead to more serious problems. Signs of infection include redness, throbbing, warmth, and obvious pus. Red streaks up the leg are a serious sign of infection, as are chills and fever. For long-distance hikers, a serious laceration requires a visit to a doctor for possible stitches and some downtime.

Frostbite

Hiking in cold weather brings with it the risk of frostbite. The hands, feet, and face are particularly at risk. Initially, when the body notes a significant decrease in outside temperature, it shunts blood away from the extremities to reduce heat loss and keep the core body temperature from dropping. This leaves the extremities vulnerable to the cold. Over time, as the extremity's temperature drops, blood is allowed back into the hands and feet in an effort to prevent freezing. At this point, they appear beet red and feel painful. If the cold persists, the exposed tissues will eventually freeze, causing death to the cells involved. Frozen tissue appears hard, white, and completely numb. If the extremity is warmed up in time, only the superficial skin will slough off. If not, deeper tissues will freeze until digits (and finally entire extremities) are lost.

Prevention, of course, is the best way to avoid frostbite. It is vitally important to keep dry, as moisture greatly increases the skin's rate of cooling and the chance of frostbite (wet clothing transfers heat 23 times faster than dry clothing). Dress in layers that will keep you warm, and since one third of heat is lost through the head, keep yours covered. A thin, wicking sock liner with a heavy wool/acrylic sock may be the best bet for your feet. If you are concerned that an arm or leg is getting frostbitten, try to place the freezing extremity next to your body core—hands under your armpits, feet under a friend's parka—and use a vapor barrier (plastic bag) over feet or hands if necessary. Moving about will also help circulation and reduce the chance of frostbite.

A Brush with Frostbite

As it turns out, I have second-hand experience with frostbite. My brother and sister-in-law were visiting Nepal during the fall of 1995–1996. They had hiked only one day from Katmandu when an intense snowstorm system developed during the night. Their guides insisted they depart immediately for the village. On the way, an avalanche cost them four members of their party and all their gear. Because of the deep snow, progress was extremely slow. By the second day, they were still nowhere near town. By this time, one of the guides was suffering from hypothermia. My brother donated some gloves, boots, and a coat, but the guide ultimately died.

The group was forced to make a life or death decision. The quickest way down was to follow the stream, but that would cause them to get wet. If, however, they were caught on the mountain another night without food or protection, they would die.

They took to the stream and finally made it to town, but my brother paid the price. He developed gangrene of all the toes and most of the fingers of his right hand. (Yes, he is right-handed.) Doctors tried medications and hyperbaric oxygen, but he ultimately lost them all. It was extremely painful. After at least six surgeries to remove the fingers and toes, remodel the skin, graft and stretch the remaining portions of his fingers, he is finally better.

Few people hike in as extreme environments as Nepal, but sudden, deteriorating weather conditions can occur throughout the U.S., creating potentially life-threatening conditions. Even in the Smokies, sudden snowstorms have been known to dump a foot of snow as late as April. If you are unprepared, you will at least be miserable, and, at worst, you could lose an extremity to frostbite. My brother was lucky he only lost what he did. It could have been much worse.

Raynaud's Disease

Raynaud's disease is a circulatory disorder that can be triggered by cold. It is more common in females than males. It is considered a vasospastic disorder, meaning it causes the tiny arteries in the fingers and toes to temporarily clamp down, shutting off blood flow. The fingers or toes can turn white, become painful, then turn blue, and ultimately turn red (patriotic colors) as the arteries relax and blood flow returns. The reduced blow flow can be triggered emotionally, so panic is not helpful. Stay away from vasoconstrictors like nicotine, which constrict blood vessels. On the trail, gentle warmth and time will return the circulation. In some people, Raynaud's is a sign of a serious underlying medical disorder such as lupus or rheumatoid arthritis. Your physician should determine if this is the case.

If at all possible, find shelter and drink lots of hot fluid. Both alcohol and tobacco inhibit the body's ability to deal with the cold, so they should be avoided. The belief that drinking alcohol will "warm up the bones" is a myth. It is a vasodilator (meaning it widens the blood vessels) and will cause you to lose body heat faster.

TREATMENT: If you have frostbite, treatment depends a lot on how long it will take you to extricate yourself from the cold. The absolute worst thing you can do is rewarm frozen tissue and have it refreeze. This will certainly result in the loss of tissue. Try to keep off a frozen foot, but if you must walk, be as careful as possible to avoid injury. **Do not** rub snow on a frozen body part; in fact, don't rub frozen tissue at all. This will cause damage to the skin. To rewarm a frozen part, immerse it in 100–105°F water. Do not use water that can scald. Since the area is numb, it is easy to turn frostbite into a scalding burn by using water that is too hot. Seek medical attention as soon as possible to preserve what tissue is still viable. Aspirin can be helpful to prevent thrombosis (clotting in the small arteries), but narcotics may be required for pain.

Of course, the risk of generalized hypothermia—or core temperature dropping below 95°F—should be addressed as a life-threatening injury. Extreme shivering, hallucinations, lethargy, confusion, and finally coma and cardiac arrest can occur with hypothermia. If you come upon someone in this state, do your best to rewarm him/her, but get them to a place of safety quickly. That is your primary job. Then seek professional medical help. For more information on hypothermia, consult a medical first aid text.

Sunburn

This is one burn that's quite common but infinitely avoidable. There are plenty of sunburn products available everywhere, which are rated by their sunburn protection factor (SPF). Basically, you want a SPF of about 15; anything more may just be advertising hype. SPF 15 will let you spend 15 hours in the sun while experiencing a one-hour dose of UV exposure. Of course, sweating and the thickness of a product's application have some effect. Reapply sunscreen to your face occasionally during the day. There are a few different chemical sunscreens: PABA works well despite its recent negative publicity; newer sunscreens use cinnamates, salicylates, and Avobenzone; and for complete sun block, use zinc oxide paste, especially on sensitive parts of the face. The best protection, however, is clothing—especially a hat.

UV intensity is greatest between 11 a.m. and 4 p.m.; either keep out of the sun during those times or take extra precautions. Keep in mind that even in the winter, sunburn is possible from reflection off snow, and that elevation can also be a concern: for every 1,000 feet of elevation, you increase UV exposure by 4%.

Certain drugs can be phototoxic. This means that some prescription medicines react with sunlight to cause a skin eruption. There are over 240 known drugs that can react with the sun. They include certain oral diabetes medicines, NSAIDs (Non Steroidal Anti-Inflammatory Drugs), antihypertensive medicines, antidepressants, tetracycline-type antibiotics, some antihistamines, cholesterol-lowering medicines, quin- olone antibiotics, and others. As you can see, the list is extensive. The chances of a drug reaction with the sun are small, but you should discuss the risks with your physician and take precautions. You should not discontinue any prescription medication without consulting your physician!

TREATMENT: For mild sunburn, use cooling compresses, aspirin, or NSAIDS, stay out of the sun and drink fluids. Then use a good skin cream to soothe dry, peeling skin. Some vitamin A and vitamin E in the cream is beneficial. That peeling skin, by the way, is the dead skin burned by the sun. I personally find aloe of little benefit, and would not recommend calamine for sunburn. Topical anesthetics are almost useless and may actually aggravate the skin. In the event of a very significant sunburn, see your physician. It may be a radiation burn caused by UV rays. UV radiation is filtered by the ozone layer of the atmosphere. Pollution, including Freon-type chemicals (chloroflurocarbons), is thinning this layer rapidly. It has been predicted that the northern hemisphere will see a 5% reduction in ozone in the next 10 years. Each 1% reduction will cause a 1–2% increase in skin cancer. Ultraviolet light has been arbitrarily divided into three ranges—UVA, UVB, and UVC, depending on the frequency. DNA, our genetic code, absorbs ultraviolet light at the 300nm frequency. This is in the UVB range, and that's why you see ads for UVB protection. Do not be mislead—UVA can also cause damage. Common skin cancers, such as basal cell and squamous cell, are easily treated if detected early enough. Melanoma cancer is very dangerous and often deadly. You should examine your own skin for any changes in freckles, moles or birth marks, etc. and bring them to you physician's or dermatologist's attention. Bad sunburns when you are young put you at greater risk for developing cancer as an adult.

SKIN DISORDERS

Fungal Infections

These occur in a variety of ways and places, all of them irritating and possibly painful. Athlete's foot and jock itch are the best known of these infections; candida is less well known.

Athlete's foot can be exquisitely uncomfortable. For more on this, see below under specific foot injuries. Jock itch is a fungal infection of the groin. There is redness, perhaps blisters, itch, and pain. Treatment consists of topical antifungals and drying powders. Lamisil (OTC) is also an excellent treatment for jock itch, but you must keep the area as dry as possible—fungus thrives in moist, warm areas.

Candida is a yeast infection common in warm areas, particularly in the skin folds. People with diabetes are most susceptible to candida, but anyone can get it. Symptoms usually include a red patch with white-draining pustules in the skin folds—no fun. Luckily, there are effective topical candida medications. Do not use any cortisone creams on fungal infections. It is like fertilizer to them. They will grow luxuriantly and so will the symptoms. There are many OTC candida medications for vaginal infections. First-time infections should be examined by your gynecologist or physician.

Another problem, prickly heat, has similar symptoms to fungal infections—red skin, very tiny blisters, and quite itchy skin—but is caused by blocked sweat ducts. Common in warm, humid areas, prickly heat is best treated with drying agents, powders, and soothing lotions.

Rashes

Rashes are often allergic reactions to either a chemical, insect bite, plant sap, boot material, sweat, or some other irritant. Some feet are prone to dermatitis from the chemicals, glues, and leather dyes in hiking shoes. The warmth and sweat leaches these chemicals out, initially causing an itchy rash that may blister, weep, or redden. If it continues, a dry, cracked lesion will form.

It is important to determine what you are allergic to by the use of a patch test from your doctor; then try and eliminate the offending chemical. Reducing sweating with a topical antiperspirant for the feet will help, as will foot soaks with Epsom salt or Burows solution. Sometimes, only a prescription cortisone cream will help. These lesions will seldom respond to OTC hydrocortisone.

With mosquito bites, the only thing that will stop the itch is to **stop scratching it!** The itch is an allergic reaction to a chemical in the mosquito saliva that prevents blood clotting. It will dissipate quickly if let alone.

If you have found a good topical medicine for mosquito bites that works, let me know, because I haven't found one. The problem is that the skin is designed to be a barrier to all chemicals. It works so well that topical anesthetics, like benzocaine, and topical antihistamines do little because they can't penetrate the skin.

Psoriasis

Psoriasis is a complex disease that has significant effects on the skin and can produce symptoms that range anywhere from mild dandruff and skin flaking to debilitating arthritis. Commonly, symptoms include silvery-white scales and salmon-pink skin in affected areas. Elbows and knees are most common locations, but a form of psoriasis does affect the palms and soles of the feet, appearing as tiny pustules. The toenails can also be affected, and appear pitted with yellow brown spots underneath and a lot of debris under the nail. These symptoms can be confused with fungus, which is why a nail culture is important before using an antifungal medicine.

TREATMENT: There are successful treatments for psoriasis but no cures. A combination of UVA light and certain topical creams such as retinoids works well. Nails can be debrided by a podiatrist for relief. Unless your psoriasis is acutely active, it should not stop you from hiking. Psoriasis's arthritic effects are discussed under arthritis.

Warts

Warts are a viral infection caused by the *Papilloma* virus. While they may look like corns, they are not the same. Warts grow and spread and are quite the nuisance. They are painful to hikers and easily picked up in the same places you might get an athlete's foot infection—gym, shower, pool, etc. Plantar warts are not special warts, just warts on the sole of the foot. If you think you have warts on your feet, get rid of them ASAP, before they get too large. I have seen warts the size of a half-dollar. It took almost nine months to destroy them.

TREATMENT: OTC medications may work, but often a doctor must be called in to eradicate warts. If you want to try OTC first, use Mediplast, Salactic Film, or Duofilm; these are all OTC salicylic acid preparations designed to "burn" the wart. They work but are slow, so be patient— they can take up to two months. Remember, **do not** use these medications on corns and calluses, which are caused by mechanical pressure, not an infection. Medications intended to treat warts will not work on corns or calluses!

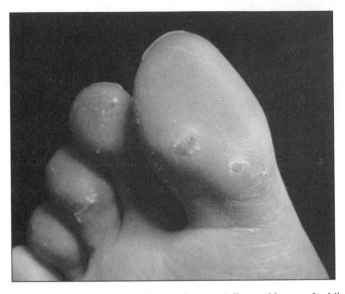

Warts on the toes or soles of the feet can be especially troublesome for hikers.

Occasionally, surgical excision of warts may be necessary. Lasers can be used to destroy plantar warts. I do not believe they offer any advantage over more traditional destructive techniques. You are still left with a "hole" that can take weeks to close. Surgical techniques may also lead to scarring. A scar on the bottom of the foot may be painful for the rest of your life, so surgery is not a preferred method of treatment There is at least a 5% recurrence rate for all wart treatments.

MUSCULOSKELETAL PROBLEMS: BONES, JOINTS, LIGAMENTS, MUSCLES

Fractures

There are two types of fractures—stress fractures, resulting from continual repetitive pressure; and fractures resulting from sudden trauma.

It is almost impossible to self-diagnose a stress fracture, though other fractures can be a little easier to diagnose. Obviously, the most extreme fracture is a compound fracture, where the bone penetrates the skin. Fractures that penetrate the skin should be considered medical emergencies—remember the ABC's (Airway, Breathing, Circulation). In the event of a simple fracture (i.e. the bone does not penetrate the skin), look for an obvious malposition of a limb or pinpoint pain over a bone. If you gently press in this spot and feel a crunching sensation (called crepitus), the bone is broken. Another indication is the guarding of the affected part by the victim. This behavior has given rise to the old wives' tale that a broken part cannot move. You can move a broken limb or walk on a fractured ankle, for example (granted, with a great deal of pain).

Fractures that cross a joint may not be medical emergencies, but they should be considered quite serious. Significant arthritis can develop from a fractured joint because the joint's articular cartilage is also damaged. After a short period of immobilization, range-of-motion exercises are an important part of rehabilitation to help maintain joint function.

TREATMENT: General treatment guidelines for fractures include immobilizing the affected area, decreasing weight bearing, applying ice, and elevating the injured body part. Unless you know exactly what you are doing, splint the fracture as it is; do not attempt to set the fracture. The first rule of medicine is "do no harm!" You can tape, tie, or strap the affected part to keep it still, even if it is at an odd angle. If the fracture is due to a fall, you should also check for other injuries. Remain calm, and seek X-rays and medical care upon returning from your hike. It's a good idea to avoid aspirin—it increases bleeding—so use Tylenol or ibuprofen for pain management.

Specific fractures to the feet are discussed later.

R.I.C.E. Protocol

The R.I.C.E. protocol is the initial treatment or all musculoskeletal injuries: Rest (keep off the injured part), Ice (or cold water if available), Compression (boots compress well or use an Ace bandage), and Elevation (keep the injured part elevated).

Dislocations

Dislocations are usually caused by a fall and are quite painful. They can be reduced (put back in place), but if you don't know what you are doing, you can cause further damage when trying to help. If you don't know how to reduce the dislocation, splint it where it lies. Otherwise, you can apply traction and reverse the direction of the injury. Toes are relatively easy to reduce, while other larger joints require skill and training. Of course, medical follow-up on all significant musculoskeletal injuries is required to assess the stability of the area and the need for casting or surgery. Ignored injuries often end up with instability, arthritis, and chronic pain.

Sprains

Ligaments maintain the structural integrity of a joint; an injury to a ligament is called a sprain. Ligaments can be torn when excess pressure is placed on a joint extended past its maximum range of motion. For example, a quick misstep into a rut can cause a foot to rapidly invert faster than the muscles can react. Full body weight presses on the ligament when the joint reaches the end of its available range of motion, and the ligament tears. In general, sprains are treated with the R.I.C.E. protocol.

TREATMENT: Elastic (Ace-type) bandages don't exactly support joints as well as you may think. They do compress the area in order to reduce swelling. A four-inch wide bandage is good for ankles or knees. Basic guidelines to wrapping include starting distally from the injured part and wrapping up towards the heart. Put moderate tension on the wrap, but not enough to impair circulation. Overlap turns by one-third to one-quarter depending on the compression and support needed (more overlap produces more compression and support). Anchor the end with either the clips or tape. You can even stick an ice bag underneath the wrap if one is available.

To restrict movement across a joint, a figure-eight works well. For the knee, flex the knee slightly, start wrapping on the distal side once around, go above the knee, once around the thigh, and then continue figure-eight loops. Do not go over the kneecap. Leave the kneecap free to move, but do go on either side of it. Try to avoid the crease behind the knee, as this will be irritating when walking. For an ankle, start at the ball of the foot, leaving the toes free, keeping your foot at a 90° angle to the leg; criss-cross the ankle up to the mid-calf if length allows. The heel may be left open.

Bursitis

A **bursa** is a fluid-filled sac that acts like a shock absorber between the bones and moving structures, such as tendons, as they pass over bones. The foot and the knee have many normal bursas. If they get inflamed, usually due to overuse, they can burn, throb, and limit the ability of the joint to move.

TREATMENT: General treatment includes R.I.C.E., and occasionally a cortisone injection and NSAIDS. If there is a biomechanical cause of chronic bursitis, an orthotic may be helpful. On the trail, you can pad around an inflamed bursa with felt. Cut out a U-shaped pad and place it around the painful area. There are also special silicon dispersion pads available.

Tendonitis

Tendons—very strong fibrous bands that attach muscles to bone—can be overworked and cause symptoms similar to bursitis. They glide smoothly in a near-frictionless sheath, but overuse causes friction to develop between a tendon and its sheath, creating inflammation and pain. Tendons can also experience chronic irritation where they pass over a bony prominence. The Achilles tendon is a prime example. It rubs against the back of the heel, and a boot pressing from the outside can aggravate the situation. A tight or contracted tendon is more prone to tendonitis.

TREATMENT: General treatment is the same as for bursitis—ice, NSAIDS, and possible immobilization of the surrounding joints to rest the tendon.

Cramps

Heavy-duty use of your muscles can cause cramps. These may occur while hiking or afterwards. They can even wake you up at night. There are many causes of muscle cramps, including fatigue, dehydration, electrolyte imbalance, certain prescription medications, and varicose veins. Pregnancy increases the possibility of cramps.

If, when walking a few blocks, you get a cramp that releases after a minute of rest, you may have poor circulation. This is called intermittent claudication and occurs when the oxygen needs of the muscles are not met by circulation. Lactic acid builds up in the muscles and they cramp. If you experience intermittent claudication, you should check with your physician. There are medicines that may help with the symptoms, such as

Trental, but they do not actually increase circulation. They make red blood cells more "slippery," or able to squeeze into partially blocked arteries. However, the **only** way to increase circulation is to **walk,** and where better than on a trail? If you have intermittent claudication, you should walk to the point of cramping, stop for one or two minutes, then walk a little more. Over time, your distance will improve and so will your circulation—in your legs and heart both. A cramp in a muscle when sitting or in bed is not a sign of poor circulation.

TREATMENT: On the trail, prevention begins with proper stretching, frequent drinking of fluids, and intake of sodium and potassium salts (found in Gatorade-type drinks and many foods). Wearing support hose will help with varicose vein cramps. If you experience chronic cramps, your physician may want to adjust your medications and perform blood tests.

What to do when you get a cramp? While it has been recommended to knead a cramped muscle, I think you will do better by slowly stretching the muscle. Cramps are quite painful, but they will relax with gentle stretching pressure. After the cramp, take it slow because recramping is possible. If the cramp occurs when sitting or lying, your best recourse is to stand and slowly walk. This will help release the cramp.

Trigger Points

A trigger point is a hard and painful knot in a muscle that can cause pain in a different location of the body. With a trigger point, the central nervous system is confused as to where the pain emanates from—something like a crossed wire—so that not only does the trigger point hurt, but pain emanates along the nerve root attached to the trigger point.

Trigger points are common in hikers and backpackers, appearing throughout the leg, buttocks, and back, and can be caused by overuse, an accumulation of toxins, anaerobic low-oxygen conditions, excessive strain, or psychological stress. Backs are a common location for trigger-point pain, which can project down into the buttocks. Overuse, hiking with a pack, scoliosis, limb length differences, and stress are all possible causes. With experience, you can find the trigger point, release it, and alleviate the pain. You may locate them on yourself by deep palpation of a painful muscle. They often overlie a bone. You will feel a painful nodule deep in the muscle, and when pressed, pain will flare up in the knot some distance from the trigger point spot.

TREATMENT: Your best bet on releasing the trigger point is to first stretch the muscle and probe for the maximum point of pain. Once found, maintain pressure on the spot for at least 20 seconds—yes, it will be painful, but it will ultimately relax. This breaks the cycle of pain. Afterwards, a light massage of the muscle may prove helpful. There may be more than one trigger point in a given muscle, so check out the entire muscle. Other treatment techniques include ice massage with light stretching and deep massage.

There are many special back exercises to avoid or release trigger points in the back. One good stretch is performed by lying on your back, knees up, with your feet on the floor. Place one leg over the other and slowly let it pull the other leg down stretching one side of the low back, then reverse sides. Consult a chiropractor for other exercises.

Trigger points in the gluteal muscles radiate pain into the buttocks and are worsened by uphill climbing. To stretch these, lay on your back, grab your leg behind your knee, and slowly pull your knee towards your head as far as it can go without causing pain.

Quadricep trigger points can occur virtually anywhere throughout this muscle group, including the medial and lateral thigh. A specific stretching exercise for the quadriceps is performed by lying on your side, grabbing your ankle, and slowly pulling your foot up to your buttocks. "Groin pulls," or trigger points in the adductor muscles of the thigh, cause pain in the medial thigh from groin to knee. One stretch to prevent or alleviate this involves holding on to something for stability, spreading your legs as far as the pain allows, and slowly rocking your hips back and forth. You can also lay flat on your back, pull your legs up to 90°, and slowly let gravity spread them apart. It may be helpful to do this against a wall for support.

Trigger points in the hamstrings can cause pain down the back of the knee either medially, laterally, or on both sides. To stretch these out, sit with knees straight and locked. Bend from the waist and try to grab your toes. Do this stretch very slowly. Calf muscle trigger points can cause pain down the calf and medially into the arch. (See the Achilles tendonitis section on stretching.)

Anterior leg trigger points cause pain to run down the shin and into the toes. This is made significantly worse by downhill hiking because you use the anterior tibial muscle to decelerate your body as you descend. The anterior tibial muscle can be stretched by sitting down, crossing one leg over the other, grabbing your foot, and slowly plantarflexing it (pulling it down). Alternatively, you can sit in a chair, place your foot behind you so that the top of your toes are on the ground, and slowly plantarflex the foot. Using the accelerator pedal while driving can also exacerbate this muscle. The anterior tibial muscle will ultimately need strengthening exercises to prevent the recurrence of trigger points there.

A trigger point in the peroneal muscles can cause pain in the lateral lower leg. This may best be treated with foot orthotics. Too forceful a stretch can damage the ankle joint or the nerves on the top of the foot.

Trigger point pain can occur on the medial side of the leg and radiate down into the sole of the foot from the posterior tibial muscle. This is a deep muscle and not easily palpated. It is best treated with functional foot orthotics.

Trigger points can form in the muscles that run into the foot—the long flexors and extensors of the toes. These too are best treated with appropriate shoe gear and foot orthotics. A good foot massage is ideal for relief of trigger points in and around the foot.

Commonly, a trigger point can reoccur if stressed again and may require injections or physical therapy such as galvanic electrostimulation, cold spray and stretch, chiropractic manipulation, therapeutic massage, acupuncture, or other medical interventions. Muscle relaxants do not offer relief for trigger points. The relationships between muscle, trigger point, and referred pain can be quite complex and may take a physiatrist (a physical medicine physician) to sort out. Certainly, the back is an area where you do not want to self-diagnose.

Unfortunately, the best treatment for overuse injuries is the oldest treatment—time. You may relieve much of the pain with medicine, but only time will heal these "wounds."

Arthritis

Arthritis is an inflammation of a joint, and it can result from a number of factors.

The **rheumatoid** family of arthritis is a disease that affects the entire body and is best handled by a rheumatologist. This is a disease in which the body attacks itself—an autoimmune disease—and erodes the joints. The classic signs include morning stiffness, pain in multiple joints (especially the wrist and fingers), and rheumatoid nodules. While there is no cure, there are effective treatments, and depending on the severity, most people can continue an active life that includes hiking. General treatment goals include relieving pain and maintaining joint function. Keeping as active as possible will help.

Another type of arthritis, **gout,** has been dubbed a "rich man's disease," because it was thought that eating rich foods causes it. This is quite untrue. Gout is an accumulation of uric acid, which is deposited in joints. Uric acid is a byproduct of our metabolism and is not very soluble in blood. In the cooler areas of the body, uric acid crystals precipitate out into joints. This triggers a severe inflammatory response from the body. The big toe joint is the most common site, but it does impact many other joints. If you have gout, it is quite obvious. The area gets red, fiery hot, throbs, and looks angry. It can be triggered by mild injuries, so it can occur on the hiking trail. If you know you are suffering from gout while on the trail, the best thing you can do is take cool soaks (like in a stream) and OTC NSAIDS. When you get home, you will need prescription NSAIDS and/or Colchicine from your physician. The attack of gout will subside in five to seven days, but each attack damages the affected joint. There are medications, such as Allopurinol, that can reduce your blood level of uric acid to help prevent future attacks.

Psoriasis, a complex disease that can affect the joints as well as skin (see entry above), is actually a form of arthritis, and can be a severe one. Its cause is unknown, but there may be genetic and infectious components. It is usually worse in the fingers and toes, with the big joints less affected. It can also hit the lower back, especially in men. General treatment guidelines are the same for the other variants of arthritis: exercise, physical therapy, orthotics, NSAIDS, and special prescription medications.

Osteoarthritis: The Hikers' Arthritis

Everyone will get some degree of osteoarthritis as they age. The rate of joint damage is related to activity level, structural problems, accidents, weight, repetitive motions, and other factors.

Unlike the other form of arthritis, osteoarthritis is a noninflammatory form of the disease that damages the cartilage of a joint, a result

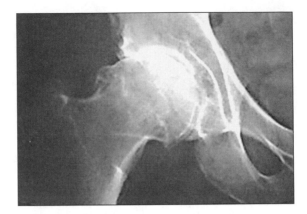

Arthritis can strike most any joint, as in this X-ray of an arthritic hip.

of the gradual wear and tear associated with walking around. Excluding severe injuries, osteoarthritis results when a joint is asked to function past its normal range of motion or when a joint has excess pressure applied to it, as in carrying a very heavy pack. Joint cartilage has virtually no ability to repair itself, so as damage to it accumulates throughout life, osteoarthritis consequently worsens. This does not mean that painful arthritis is inevitable as you age, but it is likely.

Since all the joints in the leg function as a unit, injury to one joint changes an individual's gait pattern and affects all other leg joints. This can lead to additional damage in other joints as they attempt to compensate. This is where prevention and treatment do well. If one joint is being asked to perform "above and beyond" to compensate for another joint, the situation can be addressed with therapy and orthotics.

For example, a patient injured her knee as a child and is now "knock-kneed." Her knees do not hurt, but her ankles and lower back hurt. As it turns out, the injured knee is slightly short and a little tighter than the healthy knee. This caused a limb length discrepancy, hurting her lower back. The fact that her feet were hitting the ground at an angle caused them to pronate, or flatten out. This pronation put excessive pressure on the STJ, causing arthritic pain to develop. Her treatment consisted of stretching exercises, a 1/8-inch heel lift, and a foot orthotic to stop the foot from compensating for the "knock-knee." She was able to continue hiking without pain. This is a good example of the interaction of all the joints in the legs, how they compensate for each other, and the extended damage that one injury can create.

TREATMENT: There is no cure for osteoarthritis, but very effective treatments exist to help keep you active. These include new medications, NSAIDS, physical therapy, and orthotic devices for feet, ankles, knees, and hips.

For self-treatment, try warm soaks (how about a Jacuzzi?) and OTC NSAIDS, such as ibuprofen or Aleve (if not contraindicated—ask your doctor). It's true that when it hurts, the last thing you want to do is go for a long walk; but the fact is the more mobile you stay, the better you will feel—physically and mentally. You should rest only during acute flare-ups. Start off slow, stretch, increase your pace slowly, and you can continue hiking and enjoying it.

For painful muscles, there are topical analgesics that help ease the pain. These include the liniments like Ben Gay, Mineral Ice, Biofreeze, Myoflex, and others. They are "counter irritants." These have menthol, eucalyptus, and other medications that bring warmth to the area applied. They supply very short-term relief, but by all means try them for a sore back or leg. There is a relative newcomer to the topical analgesics. It contains capsaicin, the "active ingredient" in pepper. It has been used with mild success for diabetic neuropathy and neuritic pain. Recently, it was introduced to the market as relief for muscle pain. Just be careful not to get the cream in your eyes. It is best applied thinly but often, and the results are cumulative. For neuritic pain, you need to continue using it for a month before making any judgements as to its usefulness.

NSAIDS

In the past, cortisone was used extensively to decrease inflammation, pain, and fever, but it had many side effects; in particular, it suppressed the immune system and was harsh on the stomach lining. It is still used for some chronic cases of arthritis and acute infections, and is extremely useful. But a new class of drugs, the NSAIDs, does the same thing without many of cortisone's side effects. NSAIDs is an abbreviation of Non-Steroidal Anti-Inflammatory Drug. This means that they do not contain cortisone, which is a steroid.

How do NSAIDs work? There is a whole set of inflammation-producing chemicals in the body that act to draw healing cells and fluids to areas of injury. One of these chemicals is prostaglandin. These chemicals cause the redness, warmth, and swelling found at injured sites. As a rule this is a good thing, but sometimes it needs help in quieting down. NSAIDs help inhibit the production of prostaglandin, thus reducing swelling and pain.

NSAIDs are not without their own side effects. First of all, asthmatics must be careful; people allergic to aspirin should be careful; and people with sensitive stomachs, ulcers, etc. should be especially careful, as NSAIDs are well known for causing stomach distress.

The OTC NSAIDs include the originals—aspirin, ibuprofen (Motrin and others), Naproxen (Aleve and others), and Ketoprophen (Orudis and others). You should know that acetaminophen (Tylenol and others) is an excellent mild pain reliever, but it has no anti-inflammatory properties. Discuss the use of all OTC medications with your physician before you take them.

Prescription NSAIDS are potent anti-inflammatory and pain-relieving medications. There are a great many of them. You should know that if your physician prescribes one that seems to have little effect, he or she may switch you to another until finding the best drug for your symptoms. A treatment effective for one patient may do nothing for a second patient—and may actually be harmful to a third patient. That is why medicine is an art. It is also why you should never share prescriptions with a friend. Some of the most common NSAIDS include Voltaren, Lodine, Relafen, and Daypro. You should know that all NSAIDS affect the stomach lining to some degree.

There is a new class of NSAIDS called Cox2 inhibitors. They affect the prostaglandins that control inflammation in the musculoskeletal system, but they leave stomach prostaglandins alone. These include Celebrex and Vioxx. They are much easier on the stomach but are still not 100% safe.

While you have little control over the ravages of rheumatoid arthritis, you can take positive steps to reduce osteoarthritis. One factor definitely within your control is excess weight, which can put increased pressure on your joints. This is not to say that osteoarthritis is only a disease of the overweight, but reducing a joint's load by 10 or more pounds can definitely help. Talk to your physician about your proper weight and dieting. Remember, only a combination of reduced calories and increased activity helps maintain weight loss over time. Stretching, addressing structural problems, training techniques, wearing your orthotics, and mixing in other sports (swimming provides a low-impact aerobic exercise) are other factors within your control.

For severe cases of osteoarthritis, joint replacement by an orthopedist is sometimes considered. This procedure can restore function and allow a return to hiking. This is especially true of arthritic hips and knees, but not ankles. This should only be considered after all forms of conservative care have been tried.

For those hikers with chronic osteoarthritis of the knee, there is a relatively new and exciting treatment for pain. Synvisc is an "elastoviscous" fluid very similar to a joint's synovial fluid. The job of synovial fluid is to bathe the cartilage in nutrient fluids and act as a shock absorber and lubricant for the joint. In osteoarthritis, cartilage wears and there is bony overgrowth within the joint, so that two bones grind against each other. Synvisc is a synthetic "lubricant." It is given as a series of three injections, once a week. Recent studies show it significantly reduces pain during activity and pain at night. It is not a cure, but it does supply temporary relief, perhaps up to six months. It is especially useful for those who cannot tolerate other treatments, such as NSAIDS, or who are not candidates for surgery. It is specific to knees only at this time.

There are several other types of arthritis. Just as it sounds, infectious arthritis results from a bad joint infection, while, just as obvious, traumatic arthritis results from a serious injury. Treatment for these manifestations of arthritis should be injury-specific, so consult a physician if you experience them.

Injuries from Plants

The two times plants become a concern for hikers are when eaten and when touched. Obviously, eating is not directly related to the feet and legs, but I can prescribe a plan of action for plant consumption: if you don't know for sure what it is, don't eat it. How's that for sage advice?

On the other hand, coming in contact with plants is more difficult to avoid, especially while in the woods; but you can reduce your chances of touching the less desirable plants by learning to identify them. These plants include but are not limited to poison ivy, poison oak, poison sumac, and stinging nettles. The rash resulting from contact with the first three is an allergic reaction—some people have a more intense reaction to these plants than others—while contact with nettles is a chemical reaction. An acidic substance is injected into the skin, irritating it and causing a red, painful rash.

Poison ivy can be vinelike, bushlike, or even treelike, and its appearance (color) will vary with the season. Remember the rule: "leaves of three, leave it be."

TREATMENT: As their name suggests, stinging nettles irritate a person's skin when it comes in contact with the plant. The stinging usually lasts an hour or two. To ease the pain, try mixing a paste of baking soda and water and applying it to the affected area.

The rash, an allergic reaction caused by contact with the sap of poison ivy, oak, sumac, and other plants, is not contagious. Unfortunately, it often takes a day or more for such a rash to develop, so if you suspect contact, wash the area completely and vigorously with soap and water. Note that you can carry the sap on your boots or clothes, or even your dog, and zap yourself later.

Often, allergic reactions to poison ivy appear as an itchy, blistery, thin line. OTC medications are not very helpful. Hydrocortisone and OTC antihistamines offer minimal relief. Soothing lotions, soaks, and compresses may be better. If you have a bad case, see your doctor for a high-potency prescription—topical cortisones, oral cortisone, or other medicine.

INSECT BITES AND STINGS

Mosquitoes and Black Flies

Certainly, the most common and annoying of biting insects are mosquitoes and black flies. Though ticks, spiders, scorpions, and other creepy crawlies demand a certain measure of respect in the woods, one cannot say enough about being prepared for the black fly and mosquito season.

Insect bite prevention involves wearing clothes that cover the skin, and when appropriate, netting over the face and gloves on the hands. An insect repellent is also a good idea; there are many on the market. DEET is one of the most effective insect repellents. For those who prefer something more natural, the chemical permethrin (made from chrysanthemums) is quite safe, but it must be applied to clothing to be effective. It doesn't work when applied to the skin. Combining DEET on the skin and permethrin on your clothes offers maximum protection. The chemical in citronella is also used as a repellent. Skin So Soft products have anecdotal short-term repellent effects, but the effectiveness of their active ingredient has not been documented.

What about the safety of DEET? There is some concern about its toxicity. The fact is that it is the most effective insect repellent for ticks and other insects. It is safe in moderate concentrations for almost anyone in decent health—young children excluded. Do you take a tiny chance and use DEET, or do you take the chance of getting a dangerous tick bite? Which is the lesser risk? What about the benefits of keeping mosquitoes and black flies away? Again, personal choice comes into play.

TREATMENT: One must pretty much grin and bear mosquito and black fly bites. Avoid scratching bites, which can become infected if scratched too enthusiastically. The more you scratch, the longer a mosquito bite will itch. If left alone, bites will stop itching in hours; if you scratch, you can enjoy the itch for days. Oral antihistamines can help reduce itching. Many oral antihistamines, such as Benadryl, are now OTC and are effective against itching but can make you sleepy. Topical antihistamines offer little relief

Scorpions and Spiders

Despite the fact that most biting spiders are venomous, fatalities are extremely rare. The black widow spider and brown recluse (or fiddle-back) spider bites, while potentially dangerous especially in small children, are mostly just very uncomfortable. The widow spider bite is immediately painful followed by a dull or numb sensation. Cramping, anxiety, sweating, dizziness, itchy rash, nausea, and warmth can ensue. Brown recluse spider bites are not immediately painful but become warm and itchy. They often blister and form an ulcer. Later, pain, nausea, fatigue, chills, and sweats are experienced.

Depending on where you are hiking, scorpions can be more problematic than spiders, but they are easily avoided. The time you most likely will encounter one is in the morning, when you go to put on your boots. In order to keep warm, scorpions like to shelter in boots during the night. By shaking out your boots each morning before you put them on, you can avoid most scorpion encounters. Except for the *centruoides* scorpion, most scorpions' stings are relatively harmless. Small children are more at risk. Scorpion stings are uncomfortable and can cause numbness and tingling.

TREATMENT: Local wound care for spider and scorpion stings should consist of applying ice, cleansing the affected area, and using either oral antihistamines or cortisone cream to relieve pain and itching. If systemic signs occur—restlessness, racing pulse, or weakness—hospitalization and antivenin are necessary.

Bees, Wasps, Hornets, and Fire Ants

The real danger in *Hymenoptera* (bee and wasp) stings is not their venom but in the severe anaphylactic reaction some may experience. It can take over 100 bee stings to produce a fatal poisonous response, but only one sting may produce a fatal anaphylactic response (an allergic reaction to the injected chemicals in a sting).

Fire ant stings often result in immediate burning pain lasting an hour with a resulting blister formation. There are rare anaphylactic reactions to ant stings, but in general, ice and local wound care are all that is needed.

TREATMENT: If you are not allergic to a sting, treatment should consist of gently removing the stinger, cleaning the wound with peroxide or Betadyne, ice, and taking an oral antihistamine or applying cortisone cream. To be honest, topical OTC creams may be ineffective. Therefore, a doctor's prescription may be required if symptoms are severe.

Now, if you know you are allergic to bee stings, you must carry a kit (an Ana-Kit or EpiPen) with a prefilled syringe of adrenaline (1:1,000 epinephrine) as well as an oral antihistamine. Know how to use the kit **before** you are stung! There are different methods of use, but in general you need to inject 1/2 cc of adrenaline near the bee sting, and the other half at another site. Take the oral antihistamine immediately afterwards. The injection's effects are quite rapid, and relief should be noticed in minutes. Follow up with a visit to your doctor. For sting prevention, avoid bright clothing and perfumes—maybe they make you appear as a large, yet mobile flower. Bees do not want to sting you—it is suicide for the bee— but they will attack if provoked. With a series of injections, you can get desensitized to bee stings.

Mites, Lice, Fleas, and Other Small Critters

Lice, scabies, and chiggers are minute skin parasites that use us as hosts. *Pediculosis,* commonly called "crab lice," infest hairy areas like the scalp or pubic area. They are spread by close physical contact and are usually itchy. The nits are visible as tiny grayish white oval bodies attached to a hair shaft.

Scabies are mites *(Sarcoptes)* that burrow into the skin and are intensely itchy. They are picked up by direct skin-to-skin contact or by using another person's clothes, hat, socks, etc. They are often found on the feet, knees, and sweaty areas, particularly in flexor folds such as the underarm. They are brownish red and make threadlike burrows visible under the skin. You may not experience symptoms on the trail—itching may begin as much as one month later. They often become secondarily infected with bacteria, causing crusted lesions.

Chiggers are soil-dwelling mites that hop on for a ride and a free meal. They will make you start itching immediately.

Flea bites are a common hiking nuisance. The itching is an allergic reaction. They appear as itchy, reddish bumps and possibly blisters, usually in clusters on the feet and legs. Not surprisingly, owning dogs and cats magnifies one's risk of encountering fleas. Fleas may be vectors for severe disease (bubonic plague was a flea-borne disease), but do not stay up late at night worrying about them unless you have hiked in an endemic area.

TREATMENT: Treatment for lice and scabies consists of applying a 5% permethrin cream to the entire body, with a possible second application one week later. Lindane is also used for lice, but at 1% strength. For young children, consult your pediatrician. Itching may be so intense that a prescription for hydroxyzine or other antipruritic is required. You can try the OTC oral antihistamine Benadryl—at least 50mg for adults, 25mg for children.

Chiggers should be scrubbed off, and an oral antihistamine or topical cortisone cream can be used to relieve itching.

Flea bites can become secondarily infected with bacteria, especially with the help of scratching. In the outdoors, they should be thoroughly cleansed. OTC cortisone creams are pretty wimpy and will have little effect on the itch. Oral Benadryl may help, but you may need a prescription for a potent cortisone cream and topical or oral antibiotics when you get home. You should also check your dog and your house for infestation.

Ticks

While tick attachment can produce localized infection, and it is quite disconcerting to find a tick on your own body, the real risks are the tick-borne spirochete bacteria that cause Lyme disease and Rocky Mountain spotted fever. The large visible tick (common dog tick)—which can be up to a centimeter long when engorged—is relatively harmless.

The deer tick *(Ixodes)* is responsible for carrying the Lyme disease spirochete, *Borrelia burgdorferi*. Although originating in Connecticut, it has been found nationwide. This tick is quite small—it's the size of the period at the end of this sentence. If found and removed early, it cannot transmit the disease. It is believed that it must be attached for more than one day for an infection to be transmitted. Deer ticks should be carefully removed and saved, the affected area should be cleaned, and a physician consultation arranged when you return home. Panic is optional but not necessary. Signs and symptoms of Lyme disease often include a red rash that expands and then clears in the center (a "bull's eye"). Flu-like symptoms often follow—fever, ache, muscle pain, and sore joints. Arthritis does not occur till late in the disease. These symptoms can vary among individuals. Without treatment, the symptoms will diminish over time, but the disease does not. The good news is that it can be diagnosed with blood tests and is often easily treated with oral antibiotics. The bad news is that if Lyme disease is not treated, permanent arthritic, cardiac, and neurological abnormalities will occur.

The FDA has recently approved a Lyme vaccine. Lymerix is available for people age 15 to 70 who are at high risk for contact with the

The deer tick (Ixodes scapularis), *a carrier of Lyme disease. Photo by Scott Bauer, courtesy U.S. Department of Agriculture–Agricultural Research Service.*

deer tick. High-risk individuals include those with frequent or long-term exposure to tick-infested habitats. It is up to you and your physician to determine if Lymerix is right for you. It requires a series of three injections: an initial dose, a second one month later, and another eleven months later. It is believed to be approximately 76% successful in preventing Lyme disease. This means that it is still vital to practice personal protection measures against ticks. It is unknown if the protection is permanent or if booster injections will be required. Side effects are mild and uncommon. They include local irritation from the injection and mild flu-like symptoms. This vaccine is a "work in progress" and will be improved with further research.

Rocky Mountain spotted fever is a rickettsial tick-borne disease also found nationwide. The incubation period is often up to a week after a tick bite, with symptoms of severe fever, chills, headache, and cough appearing thereafter. The rash appears on the wrist, ankles, palms, soles, and then the rest of the body. This is a nasty disease requiring strong antibiotics. If treatment starts early, little or no permanent damage occurs; but if treatment is delayed, serious permanent damage—even death—can occur. There are no vaccines available.

My advice is to be aware of these diseases; take precautions such as using mild insecticides, tucking socks over pants, staying on the trail, inspecting yourself (and your children) at the end of the day, and following up on suspected bites, rashes, etc., with your physician. But, **do not** let fear of these diseases stop you from enjoying the great outdoors. They are all treatable by your physician.

TREATMENT: An attached tick must be removed carefully with tweezers to avoid leaving the insect's mouthparts in the skin. The old wives' tales of removal include burning it with a match (not yourself) or covering it with Vaseline—but that may actually spread disease. The best way of dealing with it is careful removal. Then you can eliminate the nasty pest, as you desire. I recommend squashing followed by incineration. There are tick removal devices that you can buy. The Pro Tick Remedy and the Tick Nipper are two such devices. Don't use coarse tweezers, since they will crush the tick and may cause it to inject its load of bacteria into your skin. Grasp the tick by its head, being careful not to crush it. Cautiously pull it out, being careful not to separate the mouthparts from the body. The wound should then be carefully cleaned with antiseptic, peroxide, or Betadyne, and antibiotic cream and a bandage applied. The deer tick is so small that a physician may need to remove it.

S N A K E S

Snakebite information merits a book unto itself (and there are several). What you need to know is that although snakebites do occur, less than 15 resulting fatalities are reported yearly in the U.S. These are mostly children, the elderly, and members of religious sects that handle snakes. If you hike in certain areas of the country, you will encounter the occasional snake. Remember, snakes do not want to bite you. You are not food to them, and they will try their best to avoid you. It is only when you scare them with a wrong step that you are at risk. Rattlesnakes account for 70% of venomous snakebites, with pit vipers and coral snakes making up the rest. Luckily, even if these snakes bite you, envenomation does not always occur. Although this is not a hard rule, nonvenomous snakes tend to leave multiple teeth marks, while venomous snakes tend to leave one or two fang marks. If at all possible, try to identify the snake and estimate its size. You will know within 30 minutes if envenomation has occurred, but do not wait. Seek medical attention as soon as possible.

TREATMENT: Snake envenomation is not always extremely painful at first, but within 10 minutes, pain and swelling usually occur. There can be tingling and numbness, weakness, increased heartbeat, sweating, faintness, muscle spasms, bruising, bleeding, and shock. If medical treatment is available within 30 to 40 minutes, transport the patient as soon as possible. If you are further than 40 minutes away, immobilize the bitten limb, keep it below the heart, and remove all constrictive clothing and jewelry.

It is not recommended you use incisions to extract venom—this can cause other problems. Many experts believe that using an extractor device (such as those available from Sawyer Products) within three minutes of being bitten can help reduce the amount of venom.

Emergency medical care and antivenin therapy should be instituted as soon as possible. Exercise or exertion speeds systemic absorption, increasing the danger posed by the venom. Therefore, it is important for the patient to remain still. Though no scientific evidence proves its effectiveness, a mild constriction band can be applied two inches above the swollen area. It should be made just tight enough to slip one finger underneath with some difficulty. Ice is not helpful and may even worsen the tissue damage. It may be useful to outline the swelling every 15 minutes with a pen or marker. You may have to move up the constricting band depending on swelling.

Shock must be attended to immediately. Signs of shock include confusion, tiredness, cold or moist hands and feet, clammy skin, weak and rapid pulse, and hyperventilation. First aid treatment for shock includes keeping the victim warm and elevating the legs (unless the legs are envenomated). Stop any bleeding; check the ABCs—airway, breathing, and circulation. Give CPR as required. Shock can be fatal if not treated.

OTHER ANIMAL BITES AND RABIES

As far as animals go, if you are being eaten by a bear, I'm sorry but I can't help. (I can tell you that to prevent this unlikely event, you should know proper wild animal safety: tie up food and hang it from a tree at night, do not feed wild animals, do not annoy or pester them or get between a mother and her cub, etc.) If you are merely bitten by an animal, treat it as you would any wound—wash it with soap and water, then apply antiseptic and a bandage. If bitten, you will need to then concern yourself about rabies.

Rabies is caused by a virus that is carried by an infected mammal and spread directly through a bite wound. It carries with it significant risk of brain injury and death. The incubation period is 10 days to 1 year. There is a medical protocol for dealing with animal bites in the wild. If bitten, try to identify the type of animal and whether or not it is behaving oddly. Local hospitals know the relative risks of contracting rabies from the different animals in their area and can recommend whether rabies injection therapy is warranted. Prophylactic vaccines are available for high-risk individuals.

SPECIFIC INJURIES

Whereas the first section of the chapter focused on problems that are not specific to one area of the body, we now turn our attention to problems that occur in specific parts of the hiking engine. This chapter divides the foot and leg into segments and discusses specific injuries that hikers can sustain to each.

These injuries can be due to overuse or from ongoing biomechanical concerns. The latter sort may sometimes be corrected using orthotics, but other times surgery is necessary to create a more permanent solution.

FOREFOOT

Athlete's Foot

Athlete's foot is a superficial fungal infection that can be exquisitely uncomfortable. Besides causing extreme itchiness, it can make you feel like razor blades are slicing into your skin. Care must be taken not to get a secondary bacterial infection through the skin cracks the fungus creates. Fortunately, OTC medications, such as those containing clotrimazole (Lotrimin or Mycelex) or undecylenic acid (Cruex or Desenex), are excellent for prevention, especially if you are prone to athlete's foot. I highly recommend a squirt of any antifungal powder in the socks in preparation for a hike. For severe athlete's foot infection, however, a prescription will be needed. Recently, a very powerful antifungal prescription became OTC. The cream Lamisil is one of the best antifungals around. If you are prone to athlete's foot, it may even be a good idea to put it in your first aid kit. Lotions are better between the toes, while creams are better on the bottoms of the feet.

TREATMENT: There are a couple of actions you can take to help ease the discomfort and speed the healing of athlete's foot. Keep your feet

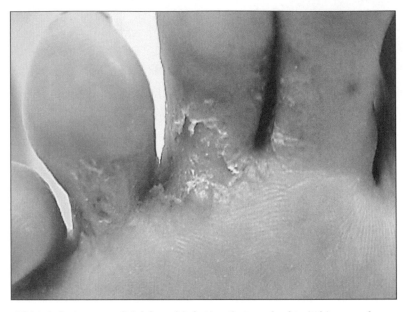

Athlete's foot, a superficial fungal infection that can lead to itchiness and sharp pains.

as dry as possible. This may mean taking a day or two off from hiking. You might want to try soaking your feet. (Believe it or not, soaking the foot actually dries out the skin.) Cool soaks with Burows solution are helpful. Old remedies of gentian violet, although colorful and messy, do work well. OTC oral Benadryl can help with the itch but may make you tired. Topical Benadryl will not be too helpful and does not kill the fungus. Do not use any caustic chemicals, such as bleach, to soak feet in. That will give you an irritant dermatitis/chemical burn that you will remember for a long time.

Blisters

If you hike, you're going to get blisters. How you deal with them, both before they crop up and as they emerge, can make the difference between a wonderful hike and an extremely painful one.

The best way to deal with blisters is to prevent them. First, **know your boots.** Never take an untried boot on a significant hike (though even broken-in boots can cause problems). Second, **know your feet.** If you have known hot spots, which are irritated on most hikes, plan ahead and place moleskin or some other product on these places before you get started.

TREATMENT: If a blister doesn't hurt, don't touch it. If the top skin is still on the blister, do not remove it. The top skin acts like a natural bandage, keeping out bacteria. If you drain a painful blister, the top skin should be left on for protection. Before starting, clean the area with Betadyne or alcohol. Take a sterilized needle, and puncture a hole just large enough to let the built-up fluid drain out. Starting away from the puncture, apply gentle pressure to the blister in order to help the fluid drain. When done draining, administer an antibiotic ointment, place a gauze square over the blister to absorb "blister juice," and cover with a large piece of moleskin or another protectant that will not shift or wrinkle when you walk. Do not place adhesive tape directly on a blister. In protecting the big toe, it is best to put the moleskin completely around the toe; otherwise, a small piece will shift and wrinkle and actually irritate instead of protect. You want any friction from the boot to be against the moleskin, not your skin. This should get you where you need to go.

Broken Toe

The toes and ball of the foot often experience problems during a hike. The most common and thankfully least serious fracture is the broken toe, one of the few injuries in this book that is strictly a result of trauma rather than overuse. It is a very painful but walkable injury and often occurs when the boots are off. This is a good reason not to wear flip-flops or sandals on a trail.

It is not always easy to know if a toe is broken. Its appearance does not always correlate with the degree of injury. In my practice, I have seen horrible, black and blue, swollen, painful toes that I was sure were broken, only to find no sign of fracture on their X-rays. Conversely, I have seen mildly swollen and minimally painful toes with a significant fracture visible on their X-rays. Don't try to second-guess any fracture. If you suspect one, treat it as such until you can seek medical attention.

TREATMENT: Treatment for a broken toe consists of taping it to an adjacent toe for support, icing it if possible, and taking your choice of an OTC painkiller. Big toe fractures are a little more serious, but all suspected toe fractures should be evaluated by a physician or podiatrist to ensure good alignment. Healing time is about six weeks.

Dislocated Toe

TREATMENT: To reduce a toe, pull the affected digit straight out with one hand, then push the base of the toe back into its joint with the other hand. Tape the affected toe to its neighbor, add ice and your choice of painkiller. If the hallux was involved, it should be evaluated by a podiatrist for stability.

Bunions

Bunions are painful "bumps" on the hallux big toe joint where it rubs against the shoe. There are a lot of old wives' tales concerning the cause of bunions—forget them all. Shoes do not cause bunions! Bunions are caused by a biomechanical problem with the way you walk. Anyone with an excessively pronated or flat foot is at risk for developing bunions. There is also also a genetic component involving bunions. While there is no such thing as a "bunion gene," you do inherit certain structural traits that predispose you to getting bunions. These include

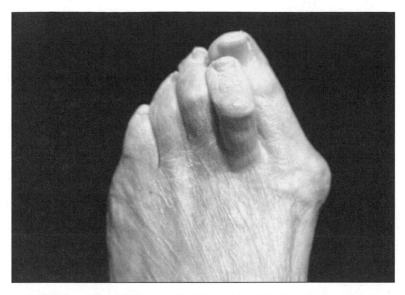

Typical bunion, a painful bump on the big toe joint. This foot also has a hammer-toe, a curled toe resulting from imbalance in the toe's top and bottom tendons.

intoed gait, knock-knees, bow legs, tight calf muscles, and intrinsic foot deformities. Bunions can only be "cured" surgically, but they can be prevented! If you have a family history of bunions and you notice them beginning on your feet, custom-made functional foot orthotics can improve your gait and help prevent bunions' development.

What if you already have a bunion? There are many good pads on the market to ease the friction on bunions. For example, Dr. Scholl makes a Cushlin soft-silicone bunion shield. You should know that absolutely **no** device with springs, levers, straps, or the like can reduce a bunion—no way, no how. When you walk, at least 150% of your body weight goes through your big toe joint on each step—you can do the math. Now what good can a wimpy, elastic strap with some medieval torture device do against that force?

You can live with a bunion in relative comfort, but if the pain gets too severe, if the joint stiffens and becomes arthritic, or if it limits your ability to work or enjoy hiking, then consider a surgical correction. There are many procedures available today, depending on the severity of the bunion; you should discuss these options with a podiatrist or orthopedic surgeon. My advice: get all your questions answered to your satisfaction and make an informed decision.

Calluses and Corns

Chronic areas of friction or high pressure produce corns and calluses—the skin's response to excessive pressure. Calluses are thickened layers of skin that act as protection against additional friction. It is only when they get too thick that they become painful.

Calluses on the bottom of the foot can be padded using either moleskin or an OTC pad such as Dr. Scholl's Cushlin transparent silicone **non-medicated** pad. Excessive calluses on the soles caused by increased pressure from a metatarsal often develop an underlying bursitis. This causes the pain and burning associated with calluses. While I don't recommend you take a knife to the bottom of your foot, a podiatrist can safely remove a corn or callous for you. Be warned, however, that this does not cure a callous. With chronic excess pressure, they will reform.

On the other hand, a corn is a deep nucleated lesion. When you have one, it's much like walking on a rock. They occur on the soles of the feet or on toes. Again, prevention is the key, but if they start to "act up," your best bet is to pad them as you would with calluses. Again, **never** use a corn-removing chemical. They are all acids and will **burn** your skin—no fun at all on a hike.

Corns can also grow between the toes. These are called "soft corns" because moisture between the toes keeps them soft. They are caused when a bone in one toe rubs against a bone in the adjacent toe. The skin becomes inflamed, thickens, and a corn develops. This type of

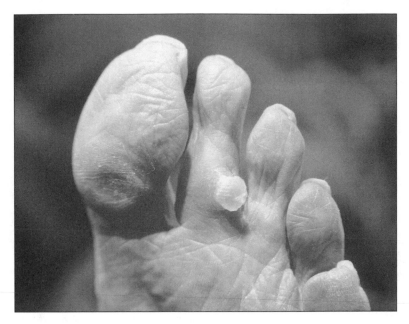

A "soft" corn, a lesion created by toe bones rubbing together.

corn is susceptible to infection, especially if you try an OTC corn re-
mover. The corn should be debrided (pared down with a scalpel) by a
podiatrist before any hike. In the outdoors, treatment consists of sep-
arating the toes with something like cotton, gauze, foam, etc. If this
painful problem becomes chronic, it can be surgically corrected by a
small in-office procedure. One of the offending bones in the toe must
be remodeled for long-term relief.

TREATMENT: To prevent calluses and corns, wear shoes that do not rub
against the toes, and use shoe inserts or orthotics to lessen pressure on
the ball of the foot. If you have a biomechanical fault causing excessive
pressure, an orthotic can help. On the trail, a U-shaped felt pad around
the painful spot will help. Foam pads are too flimsy and flatten out almost immediately. If corns or calluses are allowed to get too thick, the

When Surgery is Needed

Surgical procedures that can eliminate a chronic, painful corn or callus should be considered if the pain is debilitating enough. A painful hammertoe can be straightened out by removal of a small piece of bone, a bunion can be remodeled, or a metatarsal can be cut and put back into correct alignment if the symptoms are severe enough.

My advice to my own patients on foot surgery, in general, is that if:

1) a problem significantly interferes with work or enjoyment of a sport or exercise program like hiking,

2) all conservative treatment has been attempted,

3) your medical health is acceptable,

4) you understand completely the procedure, risks, benefits, and postoperative care, and

5) you can take the necessary time off from work and sport,

then by all means consider having the surgery. Remember that a procedure is always your choice, not the surgeon's. It is your foot, so make sure you have all your questions answered to your satisfaction. If you are willing to take the risks involved to achieve the resolution of a painful problem, then go for it.

---

underlying live skin layer will die and an ulcer can form. It is especially important that this is not allowed to happen to a diabetic.

Hammertoe

Shoes are not the cause of hammertoes; they result from a biomechanical condition. Both an excessively high-arch foot and a flat foot can develop hammertoes, which occur when there is an imbalance between tendons on the top and the bottom of the toe. When this happens, the toe starts to curl up, then rub against the shoes, causing painful corns.

TREATMENT: These corns can be debrided (pared down) by a podiatrist, extra deep shoes can be worn, and severely painful hammertoes can be straightened by surgical procedures. In surgery, podiatrist or orthopedist must anesthetize the toe, and remove a small piece of bone to allow the toe to straighten out. Simply releasing the contracted tendon has a very poor success rate; you must do something to the bone. Healing time is at least three weeks.

You should know that no OTC gadget can straighten out a toe. You can pad a hammertoe with a felt, foam, or silicon sleeve. What you might try to alleviate corns resulting from a hammertoe is removing your shoe's insole and either cutting or filing down the insole's toe end. This will give your toes an extra one-eighth inch of room in the shoe.

N A I L S

Nail problems are a common source of grief for hikers. Remember, for prevention, keep the nails trimmed short, and cut them straight across. Do not dig out the corners; that is a sure way of ending up with an infected, ingrown nail.

TREATMENT: Nails are considered relatively dirty areas of the body in terms of bacteria, so any cut, laceration, abrasion, or foreign body around or under the nail should be cleaned and dressed carefully. Betadyne and OTC antibiotic cream can be used. Nails that are partially lifted off their bed or are loosened should be similarly cleaned, and if you are hiking, keep them bandaged until you get home.

Contusions

One common nail problem is a contusion that causes bleeding under the nail. This can come from an acute injury, such as dropping a heavy object on a toe or being stepped on, but it can also occur as a result of chronic shoe pressure. This is the case when the shoe is too tight, the nail is too long, there is too much downhill walking (jamming the toe into the shoe), or if the toe itself is bent (see hammertoe above). As the injury bleeds, it separates the nail from its bed, causing pain from the intense pressure.

TREATMENT: If the pain is severe, this field technique can be used. To relieve the pressure, heat a paperclip-type object and slowly, carefully, puncture a hole through the top of the nail, letting out the blood. Try to keep the nail plate on—it protects the damaged area. Then clean and bandage the wound with your first aid kit. (You did bring one, didn't you?) This should rapidly reduce the pain. If the nail remains on, it will take up to six months for the dried blood underneath to grow out. Most often, a badly injured nail will ultimately fall off when a new nail underneath starts to grow out. This may occur weeks or months after the initial injury. If the loosened nail becomes painful, a podiatrist can remove the injured nail under local anesthesia. You should know that once a nail is badly injured, it often grows back irregular, thickened, wavy, etc.

Ingrown Nails

Ingrown nails should be dealt with before any hiking. If you have a chronic ingrown nail, a podiatrist can remove the nail corner permanently with a simple surgical procedure. The old wives' tale remedy of cutting a V in the center of the nail is a waste of effort. Stuffing cotton into the nail groove is also not beneficial.

TREATMENT: If, on the trail, a nail starts to become irritated, your best bet is not to attempt any "self surgery," for you are sure to leave a piece of nail embedded in the skin. Soaking, antibiotic cream, and a **non**-plastic Band-Aid may help. (I don't recommend plastic Band-Aids because the foot gets too sweaty. Flexible fabric Band-Aids are much better.) Even oral antibiotics are not terribly helpful, because as long as the nail is cutting into the skin, every step slices the skin, keeping it open. A podiatrist must extract the nail from the skin to allow healing. Then, if necessary, an oral antibiotic can work. I do not recommend any OTC "outgrowing medicines" for ingrown nails.

Thickened Nails

Another common complaint is thickened, painful nails. These have many causes. Either a nail bed injury or a fungus can cause an irregular nail. Psoriasis also affects the nails. If the nail is thick, yellow, and crumbling, it may have a fungal infection. A culture should be performed on the nail to accurately diagnose the fungus. You should know that OTC topical liquids applied to the nail have little chance of "curing" the fungus. Only prescription medications are successful in eradicating the fungus in a nail. A new generation of oral antifungals is now available from your doctor. Sporanox and Lamisil have been approved by the FDA for nail care. They are relatively safe and fairly effective, but they are quite expensive. It is recommended you have a blood test after one month of taking these medicines to ensure no significant side effects are occurring. Although uncommon, they may upset your liver. Patients with known liver ailments and those taking certain prescription drugs may not take these medicines. A three-month treatment period is needed to eradicate toenail fungus. A new topical medicine, Penlac, has appeared on the market. It is best used in mildly affected nails. It has only moderate success but is quite safe, with almost no side effects. It needs to be used for nine months and is also pricey.

TREATMENT: Conservative treatment of thickened, painful nails includes keeping the nails short and thin—usually with the help of a nail grinder. A podiatrist can perform this task if necessary, and should perform routine nail care on diabetic patients or those with poor circulation. As a last resort, a chronic, painful nail that interferes with work or hiking enjoyment can be removed permanently with a small surgical procedure. Under local anesthesia, the nail plate is removed and the root is destroyed with a chemical. There is no cut in the skin, no stitches, and minimal post-op pain. A toe can take two to three weeks to heal, but the procedure has a high success rate. There will be normal skin where the nail used to be. Having no nail does not leave the toe particularly sensitive. It is my philosophy that it is better to have a healthy nail than no nail, but it is better to have no nail than a chronically painful nail that interferes with your activities.

Bone Spurs

Sometimes, pain in the nails is caused by bone spurs in the toes. These spurs are located at the very end of the toe and point straight up. The nail bed is squashed between the bone spur and the nail. Add to that shoe pressure, and you get one painful toe. Sometimes, spurs even "tent" up a nail in the center.

TREATMENT: To lessen the discomfort while hiking, you can thin the nail down with a file. Similar to a hammertoe treatment, you can remove the insole of the hiking boot and cut it down to where the toes start. This will give your toes an extra one-eighth inch of room. Thick socks can also exacerbate this problem. Surgically, it is relatively easy to correct this problem. Under local anesthesia, the spur under the nail can be "filed down." This will take you away from hiking for a few weeks but is a reasonable treatment for severe pain that limits your activity.

Turf Toe

This is a sprain or hyperextension of the big toe joint. The great toe gets bent back past its normal range of motion, and the capsule and ligaments around the toe are torn. To test if you have injured your toe, try to pull up your big toe. If it is very painful, and if walking exacerbates the pain, then you may have turf toe. Such hyperextension can occur while slipping, if your toes are forced upwards. A sturdy boot will help prevent this, but a running shoe sneaker may not.

TREATMENT: This taping technique will get you safely back home. First, run an anchoring strap partway around the foot. Then, using multiple strips, start wrapping tape at the tip of the big toe and end at the anchoring strip. This will minimize motion at the big toe joint and reduce pain.

Other Forefoot Problems

At the bottom of the big toe joint, there are two pea-sized bones sitting in the **flexor tendon.** They act like a fulcrum for the pull of this tendon, similar in function to the kneecap. They are called **sesamoids.** Hikers commonly injure these bones, either from ill-fitting boots—high-arched feet and hard-sole boots don't go well together—or jumping down off cliffs; both are particularly hard on these little darlings. The resulting injury is similar to a bone bruise. Soft boot insoles like those made by Spenco can help. On the trail, you can apply felt around the injured bone by sticking it either on the skin or on the insole of the boot.

You can also get a bone bruise on the heel or the ball of the foot. Wearing a flimsy sneaker on rocky terrain is a sure way to bruise the bottom of your foot. Bruised soles can be sore for weeks, so expect some discomfort for quite a while. Any significant pain could indicate a stress fracture, which should be diagnosed and treated by a physician or podiatrist. A Spenco insole may be helpful.

Less commonly, a bump develops on the side of the fifth toe. This is called a "tailor bunion." It is either an enlarged fifth metatarsal head or a normal metatarsal that has drifted out of place. Prevention

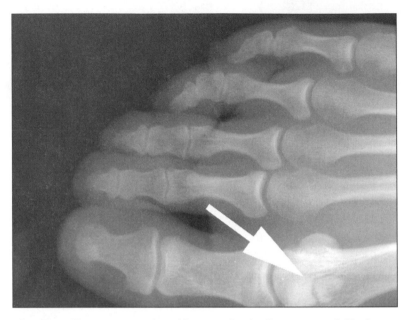

The seasmoids are two pea-shaped bones under the first metatarsal (the long bone in the foot behind the big toe). One of this patient's sesamoids has fractured into two pieces—a difficult injury to heal.

and treatment measures for tailor bunions are similar to those for big toe bunions. They include placing felt padding around the "bump," wearing wider boots, using silicone bunion pads, etc. A shoemaker can also stretch a good leather boot, making it more comfortable to hike in. Surgically, the bump can be remodeled, or if necessary, the bone can be realigned. This will keep you from hiking for a few weeks, but may be worth it if the pain is severe and no shoes can comfortably accommodate the tailor bunion.

Pains in the ball of the foot are also common in high-arch and flat feet. High-arch feet place the body's entire weight on the heel and ball of the foot; this, combined with a lack of shock absorption and a thinning of the foot's protective fat pad, causes a generalized metatarsalgia—pain in the ball of the foot. Add to this a layer of callus and an

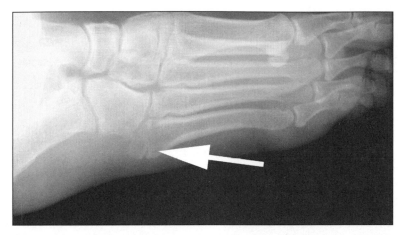

This fractured fifth metatarsal bone (the crack visible at the bottom middle of the X-ray) will keep this hiker off the trail for about six weeks.

underlying bursitis, and you can have one miserable hiking experience. Self-treatment consists of buying OTC shoe insoles like Spenco or Sorbothane. The calluses can be debrided professionally, and custom-made orthotics can be fabricated. Make sure the orthotics are designed for hiking—there are countless different types of orthotics. High-arch feet do better with softer orthotics.

On the other hand, flat feet also cause pain in the ball of the foot. Flat feet respond better to a more rigid type of orthotic. The better you can control excess pronation in a flat foot, the more comfortable it will feel. Despite the fact that they appear somewhat hard and harsh because they are custom made from a cast of your own foot, rigid orthotics can be quite comfortable. Eventually, you will not want to walk without them.

Metatarsal fractures can be caused by a direct injury or fall, but they are often stress fractures. This means they develop slowly due to excessive pressure. The bone doesn't snap in two, but it rather cracks like when you bend a live twig (hence the term greenstick fracture). The more you walk on it, the larger a fracture becomes. First metatarsal fractures should be treated with a cast from the toes to below the knee. Lesser metatarsal fractures are often just immobilized with a rigid shoe. This means that your hiking boot acts as a splint for a fractured metatarsal. If you have some felt, you may be able to pad around the metatarsal you suspect is fractured. If you are not too far from the trailhead, you can walk out with the assistance of a walking stick or your friend's shoulder—but minimize weight bearing on the foot. Continued pressure on a metatarsal stress fracture can lead to a complete through-and-through fracture, with extended healing times that require casting. Fractures in the midfoot are difficult to see on X-ray. It is sometimes necessary for a bone scan or MRI exam to diagnose a fracture in this area.

Another specific forefoot problem that needs discussion is a neuroma. This fearful-sounding condition is nothing more than an inflamed nerve running between the metatarsals. It can get pinched between the bones and get inflamed. As time progresses, scarring and thickening occur, and the pain worsens. It usually feels like a sharp stab or electric shock between the toes that may shoot up the toe or foot. A clicking may be noted when walking. Tight shoes worsen this pain by pressing the metatarsals closer together. Make sure your boots are not too tight and that you don't have on too many sock layers. On the trail, treat neuroma with massage, cold soaks, OTC pain medicines, felt metatarsal pads, and looser boots. Professional care includes injections of cortisone, shoe inserts, and ultimately surgical removal of the scarred nerve if conservative care is ineffective.

ARCH AND HEEL

Arch and heel pain may very well be the number one complaint among hikers; the two tend to be related. Often caused by a biomechanical problem, symptoms include tiredness, aching arches, and pains in the heel (especially from the first downward step in the day or after resting).

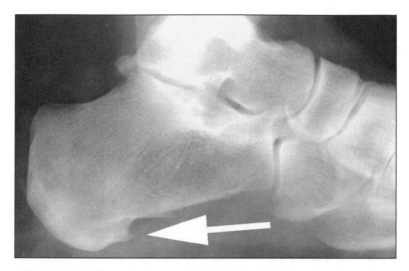

A heel spur (visible on the bottom of the heel bone) is a common cause of pain while walking.

A worn or warped shoe can worsen such a problem, but is not the cause.

Heel Spurs

There is a very strong ligament that attaches to the heel bone and flares out into the toes. This is called the **plantar fascia;** hence, arch pain is often diagnosed as **plantar fasciitis.** A flattening out of the foot puts tremendous traction on the plantar fascia. It can either tear in the middle, causing arch pain, or it can actually start pulling itself off of the heel bone, causing what is commonly referred to as a "heel spur." It is a common misconception that if you have a heel spur, the pain is coming from stepping on a sharp bony spur sticking straight down. The pain comes from the plantar fascia tearing itself off the bone. The spur—which grows out, not down—grows as a response to the chronic traction and does not, by itself, hurt. It is often most painful with the first step of the day, and then again late in the day.

The first step down after sitting can also be painful. Heel pain in a flat foot does not respond to cushions. In fact, you could strap pillows to the bottoms of your feet and your arch and heel will still hurt. What this foot needs is support—specifically control of excess pronation. Heel pain in a high-arch foot responds better to a softer, shock-absorbing shoe insert. Most boots and sneakers come with generic arches made from foam. They offer little support and little cushioning and flatten out rapidly. There is no such thing as a one-size-fits all-arch support. Everyone's feet are different

TREATMENT: If you should experience heel spurs on the trail, you can attempt to tape up the foot. This is called a "Low Dye" or immobilization strap. First, clean and dry the bottom of the foot. Next, apply one-inch medical tape around the foot from the big toe joint to little toe joint and around the heel, as an anchor.

Apply one- or two-inch tape under the arch, starting from the fifth toe side, pulling up and around to the big toe side. This should be tight. Do this from the ball of the foot to the heel. Secure the cross straps with one-inch tape around the foot, applied like the first piece. Very loosely apply one-inch tape across the top of the foot anchoring the two ends. This must be loose so as not to interfere with circulation!

This tape wrap will temporarily help support the arch. Do not leave it on more than one to two days, and be sure the top strap is very loose and not cutting off circulation to the toes. I routinely apply this strap to patients awaiting their custom orthotics and find it to be very helpful for heel and arch pain.

You may also try OTC anti-inflammatory pain medications like ibuprofen or Aleve if they are not contraindicated due to allergy, asthma, or GI disorders. Consult your doctor. A podiatrist or orthopedist may also inject an injured heel with cortisone. This can be quite effective and may provide relief for months, but it is not often permanent.

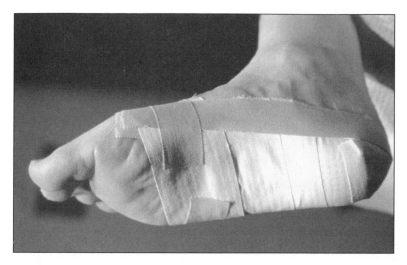

The "Low Dye" tape wrap, used to alleviate pain from heel spurs.

Long-term treatment requires functional foot orthotics that can be worn in your sneakers or boots. These are extremely effective in reducing or eliminating heel and arch pain.

If all conservative therapy fails to alleviate the pain of a heel spur, there is a relatively new surgical procedure available. Under local anesthesia, using tiny stab incisions and an endoscope, the plantar fascia is partially cut from the heel bone, allowing it to stretch. Postoperative care varies with the surgeon, but this minimally invasive procedure has a rapid healing time and often produces good results. The bone spur itself is not touched, and you will still need an orthotic afterwards. Remember, this procedure is only for patients who have had no relief with injections, NSAIDS, or orthotics and has all of the attendant risks of any surgical procedure. There is a brand-new, still-experimental procedure to treat heel spurs that uses sound waves like those a lithotripsy machine uses to break up gall stones. There are promising results, and this method may find its place in the surgeon's arsenal of treatment plans in the near future.

Achilles Tendon Complaints

There is a lot going on behind the heel: you have the heel bone, multiple bursal sacs for protection, the Achilles tendon and its surrounding structures, and finally the skin. The Achilles tendon is attached to the powerful calf muscle. It can be injured by overuse (deciding to go on a 10-mile walk after a long inert winter), chronic irritation by a boot against the heel bone, tightness in the calf muscle, or an acute injury. It can develop trigger points with radiating pain. Prevention begins with stretching before a hike and padding the heel as described above. Treatment of Achilles tendonitis on the trail includes R.I.C.E., OTC NSAIDS, and a heel lift.

Some people, especially women, have problems with the back of the heel, where the Achilles tendon attaches. This has been called a "pump bump" because certain shoes (pumps) exacerbate this in women. As the shoes rub against the heel, the back of the **calcaneus** (heel bone) becomes thickened and irregular over time. There may even be bone spurs within the Achilles tendon. This can cause considerable pain when a boot grinds the skin and Achilles tendon against the bone.

Some shoes have Achilles tendon protection built in. Such a shoe has foam pontoons on either side of the inner heel to keep the Achilles tendon from rubbing against the shoe. Silipos makes a soft silicone half-sock that goes over the back of the heel, protecting it from the friction of a boot. One-eighth-inch heel lifts in both shoes can help. Just make sure they are balanced. Ultimately, surgical remodeling of the back of the heel may be required. This requires partially detaching the Achilles tendon and has a long recovery period.

Occasionally, hikers experience what has been described as a "gunshot to the Achilles area." This is a rupture or partial tearing of the Achilles tendon or **plantaris tendon** (a little fellow next to Achilles). A misplaced jump or slip can cause this injury. It is quite painful. One

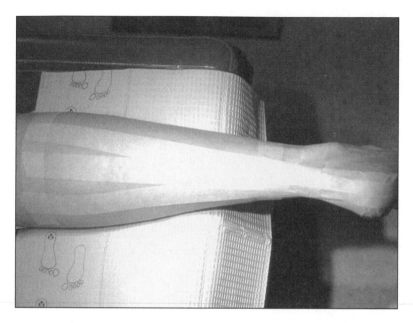

Tape wrap for Achilles tendon complaints.

way to tell if the entire tendon has been torn is to gently squeeze the calf muscle about halfway down. If the foot pulls down (plantarflexes), then at least some intact tendon remains. If you walk on a partially torn Achilles tendon, it may tear completely through; so on the trail, you must avoid all weight-bearing on that leg.

There is a taping technique for injury to the Achilles tendon. Start with the foot close to 90° to the leg in slight plantarflexion. Take one strip of tape; apply it to the bottom of the foot in the arch area and up over the heel to just behind the knee. Start another strip from the same area and angle it just medial to the first piece, so it overlaps slightly. Similarly, start a third strip in the same area and angle it just laterally, so as to overlap the first piece slightly. An anchor strap should be applied around the strips' starting and ending points without completely circumnavigating the entire leg. Then, horizontal strips should be run from the back of the heel up the back of the leg. (Again, not around the entire leg.) Finish with two vertical anchors to cover the ends of these strips. This technique should limit the ankle's dorsiflexion and protect the Achilles tendon from further damage.

It is quite difficult to break your heel bone unless you have a fall from a significant height. While not a life-threatening emergency, a heel fracture is serious and can have long-term consequences if the ankle or STJ is involved. It may need surgical reduction and/or casting for up to 12 weeks! If you have suffered a fall from some height on the trail, please check yourself out from head to toe. Lightly squeeze the heel from either side; if it is exquisitely painful, suspect a heel fracture and keep it non-weight-bearing with the help of your friend, a crutch, or walking stick. Then get X-rays ASAP.

Other Arch Complaints

Lateral foot pain can be caused by a number of anatomical structures. The most common lateral foot pain is boot irritation along the **styloid process** of the fifth metatarsal, which sticks out a bit from the foot and acts as an attachment point for an important tendon—the **peroneal brevis**. This means that peroneal brevis tendonitis can also be caused by boot irritation. The **peroneus longus** tendon crosses under the styloid process and goes medially to the big toe side of the foot. It is a major player in foot function and can develop overuse tendonitis. The resulting pain can travel up the lateral side of the leg, but not so far as the knee. Treatment for this type of lateral foot pain consists of general tendonitis treatment, possibly orthotics, and shoe adjustments.

Lateral foot pain also results from **subluxed cuboid syndrome**. The cuboid is a bone on the lateral side of the foot. Presumably, the syndrome occurs when forceful activity of the peroneal muscles pull the cuboid bone down, locking it in place. This often happens when walking over uneven terrain (flat feet increase a person's risk). If you have sharp pain over the cuboid bone while hiking, there is a chiropractic maneuver that can be performed—if you have an assistant. Lay prone on the ground, flex your knee, and have your friend place both thumbs on the bottom of the foot by the cuboid bone. By applying a quick downward thrust—like a quick snap—you can pop the cuboid back up into place. Some tape should then be applied, and an orthotic may be needed in the future.

There are also nerve entrapments in the foot—again, usually caused by boot irritation. They tend to be sharp, shooting, and radiating pains. These need to be diagnosed by a podiatrist or physician.

ANKLE SPRAINS

One of my worst hiking fears is an ankle injury. This will put a damper on any day. Most often, the foot is inverted by accidentally stepping into a hole or slipping on a wet surface, and falling with your body weight on the unstable joint. First, the ligaments around the lateral ankle will give way, the fibula bone may fracture, the ligaments between fibula and tibia will tear, and finally the tibia may fracture. Most likely, you will not be able to tell the difference between a bad sprain and a fracture.

When evaluating an ankle injury, first try to determine the direction the foot and leg were moving when injured and where the forces were. Most commonly, the sprain is on the outer (lateral) ankle. In assessing the severity of a sprain, consider the following questions:

1. Was there an immediate pain or was the pain gradual?
2. Were there any sounds—cracks, tears, or pops associated with the injury?
3. What degree of pain, swelling, and/or discoloration is present (note that the degree of swelling or bruising does not correlate well with the degree of injury)?

4. Is there any obvious deformity, bleeding, or protruding bone?

5. Can the ankle be moved up and down and side to side?

6. Is it possible to bear weight on the ankle?

Gradual pain indicates an overuse injury. Acute pain suggests a sprain or a fracture. Any sounds associated with the injury increase the suspicion of a fracture. Significant pain and swelling could indicate either a sprain or fracture—pain is not diagnostic. However, a case of obvious deformity would most likely be a fracture. It is possible to move an ankle with a fracture, although it would be quite painful. An ankle that felt unstable would indicate a serious sprain or possible fracture. As you can see, without an X-ray, differentiating between a sprain and a fracture is difficult. When in doubt, treat any ankle injury like a fracture until you know otherwise.

TREATMENT: You can make it off the trail with a bad ankle sprain or fracture if you stay cool and assess your situation. Remember the letters R.I.C.E. for all serious injuries: Rest, Ice, Compression, and Elevation. Look around for whatever is available: a walking stick, a cold compress from a stream, tape from your backpack, even duct tape (the cure-all for everything broken). Relax. Be creative, and you will slowly extricate yourself from this unfortunate accident.

If you are unlucky enough to sprain your ankle on the trail, but lucky enough to have some adhesive tape, you can tape your own ankle. First clean the skin as well as possible. Use an alcohol swab if one is available. Then run the tape from midcalf down the fifth-toe side (lateral) of the ankle (behind the ankle bone), around the heel, and up the big-toe side (medial) of the ankle (also behind the ankle bone). Start the next piece behind the fifth toe, go around the foot, behind the heel, and attach it to the area behind the big toe. Then start "basket-weaving" around the ankle, around the foot, etc. Leave the top

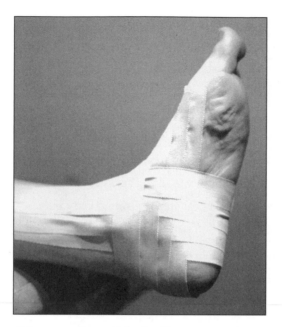

"Basket weave" tape wrap for a sprained ankle.

part of the foot and ankle open. Do not completely circle the foot or leg. When finished, run a piece of tape around the bottom of the foot and another around the midcalf to tack down the ends. Again, do not encircle the foot or leg. Your boot will also act as good support to help you walk out.

It is important **not** to ignore a mild to moderate ankle sprain when you get home. An improperly treated (or untreated) sprain can—and often does—lead to a chronic unstable ankle. This is not a rare occurrence but a real risk. You can figure an ankle will lose 10% of its strength after a sprain without treatment. If you have an easily-sprained ankle, there is a great device for prevention called an Aircast brace. It fits in a boot or sneaker, allowing up and down ankle motion but preventing side-to-side motion. This helps stabilize the ankle. Note that elastic pull-on ankle supports do not support! They may compress the ankle, but **do not** count on them to support and prevent sprains. You need a device that has a rigid support on both sides

Chronic ankle instability caused by a previous serious sprain can be improved with physical therapy, using a balance board, good sturdy boots, and wearing a splint (Aircast and others). This is good preventive medicine. Previous ankle injuries are a common cause of chronic ankle pain. That is why acute sprains should be treated aggressively and not just with an Ace wrap and some ice. A fractured ankle may require surgery to properly align and fixate a bad injury.

Other Causes of Ankle Pain

A tight calf muscle is also a major contributor to ankle and STJ pain. Stretching exercises and heel lifts, both potential solutions, have been discussed. Arthritis, also discussed above, can affect both these joints. STJ pain can be reduced with functional orthotics. NSAIDS and cortisone injections can help with the pain and inflammation of arthritis.

You have probably heard of Carpal Tunnel Syndrome in the wrist. This is a pinched nerve that sends electrical-type zaps into the hand. Well, it has a counterpart in the ankle—Tarsal Tunnel Syndrome. The **posterior tibial nerve** runs below the medial ankle and then dives into the bottom of the foot. It supplies most of the sensation and muscle innervation down there. In runs through a very tight "canal" along with its artery and vein, and it can get entrapped at this point. Symptoms of entrapment include severe, sharp, radiating electrical pain zapping into the bottom of the foot or up the leg. Initially, this comes and goes but eventually may persist most of the time. A tight boot or a mild sprain may trigger this on the trail. If the pain is mild, try to walk out with decreased weight bearing on that leg. If the pain is severe, try ice or cold water, remove the boot, and use a walking stick or a friend's shoulder for support. Professional treatment consists of injections, orthotics, and, rarely, surgical nerve decompression.

Ankle dislocation is a possible but unlikely hiking injury. Ankles do not dislocate without significant ligament or bone injury. Only attempt to reduce a dislocation if you know how or if blood flow to the foot is being disrupted.

Knee

Knee pain on the trail should be addressed in a methodical manner. The knee is too complex to self-diagnose, but you can help yourself by answering the following questions:

1. Is this an acute injury, such as a fall or a sudden twist?

2. Is this an overuse injury?

3. Does it hurt to continue walking?

4. Is there swelling?

5. Does the knee feel unstable?

6. Does the knee lock up?

An acute injury needs to be treated with the R.I.C.E. technique. An overuse injury will need rest and stretching. NSAIDS are helpful for both. An unstable knee should be taped and should bear as little weight as possible; consult with a doctor ASAP. A locked knee may have internal damage to the meniscus and will probably require surgery. Significant injury will probably require use of a knee-immobilizing brace followed by physical therapy.

Kneecap Problems

A common knee complaint centers around the kneecap or **patella.** The kneecap creates a fulcrum, allowing the quadriceps tendon to generate maximum force in moving and stabilizing the knee. A full feeling, crumbly feeling, or stiffness, especially after sitting, is a sign of "runner's knee," or Chondromalacia Patella Syndrome. This can be associated with tight hamstrings, a kneecap that does not glide in its track, severe flat feet, or other structural problems. Runner's knee can be successfully treated by quadriceps-strengthening exercises and hamstring-stretching exercises, as described earlier, and possibly functional foot orthotics to stop excess pronation. Foot orthotics work for certain knee pain because excess pronation causes a torque at the knee and STJ. This excessive knee torque can injure the ligaments around and within the knee, as well as the kneecap structures.

Cruciate Ligament Injuries

Now what about those cruciate ligament injuries that take football players out of the action for so long? The two cruciate ligaments are located within the knee joint. One tightens with the knee flexed, the other tightens with the knee extended, adding greatly to the stability of the knee. Injury to these ligaments can occur with any fall that twists the knee. There is usually a palpable snap and intense pain as the knee gives way.

To test for a knee injury after a fall, first fully extend the knee, then slowly apply pressure from both sides. Repeat this with the knee flexed. If you feel excess motion, as compared to the uninjured knee, then there may be some ligament damage. It is also possible that the meniscus, that fibrous pad between the femur and tibia, may have been torn. Bending and twisting the knee while flexed can tear the meniscus.

TREATMENT: On the trail, you must splint an injured knee, keep it from bearing weight, and consult an orthopedist ASAP upon return home. To tape an injured knee in the field, first apply an anchor tape around midthigh and midcalf (not too tight). Then apply a few strips of tape, starting mid-lateral on the calf, across the knee to the midmedi-

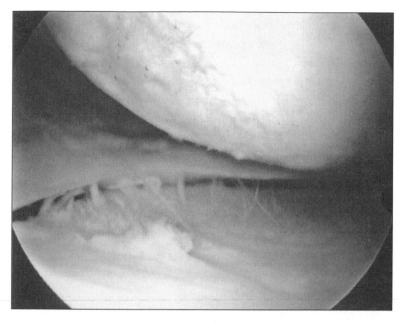

Arthroscopic picture of the inside of a knee. The femur is on top, the meniscus in the middle, and the tibia on the bottom. This knee has undergone fraying of the cartilage on the tibia due to arthritis. Photo courtesy Dr. Nestor Blyznac.

al thigh. Then apply tape from medial midcalf, across the knee, to lateral midthigh. Do not go over the kneecap. Follow with a few strips of tape from midlateral calf to midlateral thigh. You can add a few strips from medial midcalf to medial midthigh for extra support. Finish with anchor strips around the calf and the thigh to hold the strapping in place. Without an underwrap, hair is a definite problem. An Ace bandage may be a substitute option, but it will not support as well as tape.

An internally damaged knee may require surgery to repair. Arthroscopic surgery is quite successful in returning you to full activity quickly. Using two or three tiny stab incisions, a miniature television camera (arthroscope) is inserted into the knee joint along with miniature surgical scalpels, forceps, drills, and bone and cartilage tools. An adept surgeon can identify a torn ligament or damaged meniscus and repair it with

Common Causes of Knee Pain

The location of your knee pain can help determine what part of the knee you injured. Here is a quick reference chart to help you identify where the injury may have occurred. Notice that all of these injuries fall into two categories—acute injuries and overuse injuries.

FRONT

1. Patellofemoral Syndrome (under kneecap)
2. Quadriceps tendonitis
3. Bursitis

LATERAL

1. Iliotibial Band Syndrome
2. Lateral meniscus tear
3. Lateral collateral ligament tear
4. Lateral hamstring tendonitis

MEDIAL

1. Medial meniscus tear
2. Medial collateral ligament tear
3. Medial hamstring tendonitis
4. Stress fracture

BEHIND THE KNEE

1. Gastrocnemius (calf muscle) tendonitis or strain
2. Hamstring tendonitis or strain
3. Bakers cyst
4. Meniscus injury

GENERAL KNEE PAIN

1. Osteoarthritis
2. Other arthridities
3. Joint fracture
4. Injury

---

minimal trauma to the surrounding tissues. If left untreated, instability and arthritis will develop in the unstable knee.

Iliotibial Band Syndrome

Iliotibial Band Syndrome is a common runner's disorder that can also affect hikers. The **iliotibial band** is a tough fibrous band that stretches from the pelvis, across the hip, down the lateral side of the knee. Its main function is to stabilize the knee and hip while standing. Commonly, Iliotibial Band Syndrome feels like a sharp pain on the lateral side of the knee, especially when the knee is flexed while standing. It is an overuse injury caused by this tough ligamentous band snapping over the bony prominence of the lateral knee as it flexes and extends. Friction and compression eventually cause pain. There are structural problems that can cause Iliotibial Band Syndrome, such as a limb length discrepancy, bow legs, and flat feet.

TREATMENT: On the trail, carefully feel for pain just above the joint line of the knee laterally, with the knee flexed 30°. You may even feel a creaking sensation as you move the knee. Immediate treatment is standard R.I.C.E. Second, when back home, have an orthopedist rule out other possible knee problems, such as a meniscal or collateral ligament tear. He or she may suggest a cortisone injection if the pain is severe.

Your next step is prevention. Ask yourself if the problem was due to overuse: did you do too much too fast? Too many hills? Not enough stretching? Next, try and determine if any structural problems, such as flat feet, cause the pain. If so, get fitted with an orthotic. Finally, slowly return to hiking.

Here is a good stretching exercise to avoid or relieve Iliotibial Band Syndrome. Stand straight, with the limb to be stretched crossed behind the other leg. With your weight mostly on the front leg, cross the back leg as much as possible. You should feel the stretching in the lateral knee area of the back leg.

Strengthening exercises for the hip area should also accompany treatment. Using a Theraband, loop one end around each ankle, stand on one leg, and pull out on the other leg. This strengthens the hip abductors. The hip flexors and gluteal muscles need strengthening also.

With proper training, and by addressing structural problems, Iliotibial Band Syndrome can be successfully treated.

L E G

Tendonitis

Behind the leg are the hamstring tendons. They commonly develop tendonitis due to overuse. Tight hamstrings definitely increase the risk and the severity of tendonitis, so stretching, as described above, is very important.

TREATMENT: As with all tendonitis use R.I.C.E. Ice is good for 48–72 hours, then warm soaks and mild stretching. Remember, tight muscles are prone to tearing because they don't have the flexibility to recover from a mild misstep, and hamstrings are one of the most common tendons to injure.

Broken Bones

A broken leg from a serious fall may become a medical emergency. The risk of shock is great in fractures of major bones. Remember the signs: restlessness, cool or clammy skin, rapid or feeble pulse, falling blood pressure, confusion, etc. After your ABC assessment, the best first aid for a broken leg bone is to "splint it where it lies." This means that unless you are sure you know how to set a bone, don't attempt it. There is one exception. If the position of the fracture is such that the nerve or artery is being pinched off, then the limb is in immediate danger and you must attempt to set the limb straight. The best advice for setting an injury like this is figure out the mechanism of the injury and reverse the motion with applied traction. In other words, if the lower limb is angled inward, slowly apply traction and reverse the direction of injury

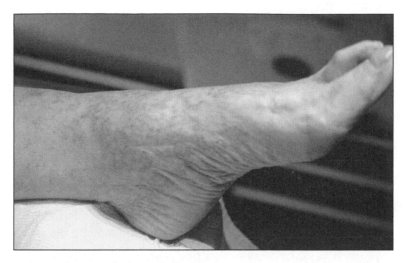

Varicose veins, caused when excessive blood pressure expands veins beyond normal size.

by moving the distracted part outward. Otherwise, using whatever is available to maintain the angle of the fracture (duct tape?), tie the limb to some rigid object like a branch, walking stick, ski pole, etc. Elevate the limb, keep the patient warm, look for signs of shock, check for other injuries (especially spine injuries), and reassure the patient.

For the senior citizen hiker, hip fractures are especially common and should be suspected in any fall that results in pain in that area.

Varicose Veins

Varicose veins appear when excessive pressure in the venous system balloons certain veins beyond their normal size. This pressure occurs when valves in the veins that normally prevent blood from flowing backward no longer function properly. With incompetent valves, blood that should continue moving up the leg toward the heart doesn't do so; the force of gravity sends blood back, pooling it in the lower leg and increasing pressure inside the veins there. The more pressure within a vein, the worse its valves work, which only increases the pressure, stretching the vein more and making the valves less effective. A vicious cycle develops. Varicose veins can be troublesome on the trail if not attended to.

Most simple varicose veins require little treatment. However, an inflamed vein should be treated or phlebitis (an inflammation of the leg veins that can lead to blood clots) may develop. Symptoms for phlebitis include aching, fatigue, heaviness, and heat.

TREATMENT: Treatment for varicose veins includes wearing compression stockings, elevating the legs, and taking aspirin (if tolerated). An Ace bandage—not wrapped too tight—will work in a pinch, but if you know you have varicose veins, get a pair of support stockings. Both OTC and custom-made stockings come in different compression strengths. If your varicose veins extend to the knee, you will need a support stocking that extends above the knee, or even up to the groin. Compression is measured in mm Hg, or the number of millimeters the pressure would push up a column of mercury on a pressure cuff or other such device. For mild varicosities, a compression of 18–25mm Hg is sufficient. For significant varicosities, you may need compressions up to 35mm Hg. They must be put on first thing in the morning, before you even get out of bed, and removed at night. After a maximum of six months, they stretch out and must be replaced. They will take some time getting used to, and, admittedly, are not any fun in the heat. Your physician can help you decide which support stocking is right for you. They are the only nonsurgical way of dealing with the symptoms of varicose veins, and they can stop the progressive, vicious cycle of varicose. They are not to be used with severe arterial vascular disease, acute deep venous thrombosis, or uncontrolled congestive heart failure.

One symptom of varicose veins is their itchiness. This is a dermatitis and is best treated with cortisone creams, either OTC or prescription. Also, an injured varicose vein can bleed excessively. If the skin is unbroken, it will bleed under the skin, forming a large bruise. If the skin is broken, it will bleed externally. Do not panic. With direct pressure it will definitely stop, though it may take a while. Apply a gauze and compression bandage with your Ace wrap and stay off the injured leg as much as possible. If heavy bleeding from varicose veins is a chronic problem, consult a vascular surgeon for possible injection therapy or "vein stripping."

If phlebitis develops, it can be a serious medical condition. There is marked pain, swelling, redness, and a great heaviness in the leg. Patients state that the calf can "feel wooden." The affected vein may bulge and feel like a cord. Elevation, compression, and warm compresses are the field treatment. This condition needs to be evaluated by a physician. It carries the risk of pulmonary embolism if left untreated.

Shin Splints

Shin splints are an overuse injury common to hikers (and runners). This is a poorly defined injury, but it usually includes pain and soreness either in the anterior tibial muscle in the medial shin or the deeper posterior tibial muscle in the medial calf. (One of the posterior tibial muscle's jobs is to support the arch. Hence, a flat foot can cause this type of shin splint.)

Shin splints are considered a **myositis** or muscle strain. Hills, flat feet or another biomechanical fault, worn shoes, and a relative weakness of the anterior tibial muscle versus a tight calf muscle are responsible for anterior shin splints. Remember, the anterior tibial muscle is the foot decelerator, stopping the foot from slapping the ground. Going downhill requires the foot to reach lower with each step, causing the anterior tibial muscle to stretch further and work longer.

TREATMENT: Of course, as always, initial treatment for muscular injuries is R.I.C.E. and anti-inflammatory medications such as aspirin or ibuprofen. Stretching before and after hiking will help, particularly using the anterior tibial strengthening exercise described earlier. You may need to adjust your training techniques—increasing your mileage (particularly on hills) too much, too fast will commonly result in shin splints. If the problem continues, you may want to consider changing boots or even getting fitted with orthotics that help support the leg and relieve stress.

HIP AND LOWER BACK

Hips are prone to arthritis and fracture, especially in senior citizens. A "hip pointer injury" is caused by a fall on the hip or blunt injury. Although it is a contusion, an X-ray should be taken to rule out a fracture if the pain is significant. Decreased weight bearing, ice, and mild pain medications are all that is necessary.

Sciatic Nerve

Anyone who has experienced sciatica problems will tell you how excruciatingly painful they can be. The **sciatic nerve** is the major nerve supplying sensation and muscle control to the entire leg. It is a giant among nerves. Unfortunately, it can be pinched in many different places. A bulging or displaced disk in the low back or an arthritic spur on one of the vertebrae can impinge upon the nerve roots. The sciatic nerve can also be pinched as it passes through the muscles in the buttocks. A sharp electrical pain radiates up and down the leg into the lower back, making it almost impossible to walk. If there is nerve root damage, muscle weakness and even bladder control problems can result. This requires physician care.

TREATMENT: It is certainly possible that excess twisting, bending, and climbing on the trail can trigger a sciatica attack. There is not

Chiropractic Care

The back is definitely a "sore subject" for many hikers. The spine is an evolving structure—not quite perfected from evolution's point of view—and is the "weak link" for many people. Pain is the great motivator when it comes to going to the chiropractor. These specialists are experts in conservative treatment of the spine and helping hikers get back on their feet quickly.

The hiker and the chiropractor are intimately linked. The hiker thrives on adventure, pushing the limits of physical endurance, and the chiropractor stands at the ready to put the injured hiker "back together" again. Concurrent with the philosophy of this book, we will discuss prevention—maintaining a healthy balanced and aligned spine.

It is said "health is the absence of disease." This definition is too black and white. It might be more helpful to visualize health and disease as two momentums head-ed in opposite directions. Disease is the momentum resulting from disintegration of structure and function; health is the momentum resulting from integration of structure and function. Through proper diet, exercise, and mental awareness, in conjunction with a spine kept free from nerve pressure through chiropractic adjustments, the body remains suited for the rigors of hiking. There is a harmony between muscles, joints, and nerves that allows you to achieve your maximum physical and mental potential. Maintaining the integrity of the spine and nerves creates a wholeness that, by integrating structure and function, allows for optimum health.

Therefore, the importance of stretching back muscles before a hike cannot be overemphasized. Increasing your flexibility, balance, extensibility, and stability can only create a more rewarding experience.

much that can be done for this while on the trail. Try to slowly walk yourself out and lay on a firm mattress for a few days. Rest, ice, and NSAIDS are helpful, but muscle relaxant medications are not.

BACK CARE ON THE TRAIL: Although there are times that intense back pain may make walking almost impossible, in the event of injury there are certain chiropractic actions that you can take until professional help is secured.

Since most muscle spasms or cramps signify a shortened or contracted muscle, your goal is to gently lengthen the affected body part. If you experience a lower back muscle spasm, remember that these muscles are big and powerful. After the muscle contracts, as quickly as possible get into a non-weight-bearing position, and fully lengthen your body with your hands outstretched over your head. Continue this stretching until the spasm passes.

Another effective technique for relieving a lower or midback spasm is to let gravity naturally traction—or lengthen—your spine. If you are hiking with a partner, stand back-to-back, interlocking arms. Have your partner gradually bend forward, pulling you up so that your feet no longer touch the ground. This must be smooth and gradual, with no jerking. You can then lie on your side in the fetal position to stretch the spine.

There are some symptoms that can occur during prolonged hiking that may be indicative of more serious spine pathology. These include numbness, tingling, or burning in the back or down the leg and progressive muscle weakness or "clumsiness." These need to be evaluated professionally.

Something to keep in mind: although hiking involves mostly the lower back and leg muscles, having arm and upper body strength helps to maintain balance and control. This prevents undue stress from being transmitted to the back.

Remember that in a fall, any suspected back injury must be immobilized. Do not move the person unless their life is endangered, because damage to the spinal cord may occur.

ALTERNATIVE REMEDIES

HOMEOPATHIC MEDICINE

There are some herbal remedies that may be helpful for certain hiking injuries. Your decision to use them may depend on your personal beliefs. Peppermint, eucalyptus, ginger oils, olgas, or arnica applied topically can help with muscle cramps and spasms. Comfrey cream can be rubbed on sprains and bruises. A mixture of hyssup, cyprus, and geranium oil can be massaged into a bruised foot. A mixture of tagets, carrot, calendula, and chamomile oil can be applied to an inflamed bunion. For arthritis, some have claimed the following herbs are helpful: angelica used as a compress, devil's claw taken internally as a capsule, bogbean taken internally as a tincture or infusion, and willow, also taken internally as a tincture.

For poison ivy, after a compress of Burows solution, colloidal oatmeal (Aveeno) can be applied. Aloe vera, tofu, or watermelon rind can also be applied. The following herbs applied topically to a poison ivy rash may be helpful: black walnut extract, echinacea, goldenseal, and myrrh.

As insect repellants, calendula, goldenseal, peppermint, lemongrass, and tea tree oil are sometimes used. Lemon balm oil, lavender, and chamomile can be applied to mosquito bites. For athlete's foot, pau d'arco tea makes a good soak. Tea tree oil also has natural antifungal properties. Calendula cream is an antiseptic that promotes the healing of skin injuries. Lavender and chamomile can be applied to sunburn. Excessive sweating may be treated with a combination of talc, lavender, rosemary, and chamomile. You can also try a soak with lavender, eucalyptus, and peppermint in water.

Glucosamine and chondroitin sulfate are two oral nutritional supplements that are used to combat osteoarthritis. While they have been around since the 1960s, they have recently been popularized. They are marketed as "chondroprotective agents." Glucosamine is a precursor to glycosaminoglycans, a component of hyaline cartilage. Chondroitin sulfate is an abundant component of hyaline cartilage. Together, they are thought to enhance production of synovial fluid, stimulate collagen production, inhibit degenerative enzymes, and allow for repair of injured cartilage. They may have mild anti-inflammatory properties. There have been many clinical studies done indicating glucosamine and chondroitin sulfate provide some benefits to osteoarthritis sufferers, with mild potential side effects. But, as with most nutritional supplements, their quality and potency can vary. They are not regulated by the FDA. They should not be used in children, pregnant women, or patients on anticoagulants. Diabetics using them should watch their blood sugar carefully.

In my clinical experience, glucosamine and chondroitin sulfate do not work for everyone, but many patients using them have experienced significant relief with virtually no side effects. The average dose is 1.5gm of glucosamine and 1.2gms of chondroitin sulfate for a 150-pound person. My advice is to try them and see. If they can help keep you active and on the trail, then do it! However, these medicines in a topical cream, in my opinion, are worthless.

ACUPUNCTURE

Acupuncture is an ancient Chinese healing art that can be of help to the pained hiker. The techniques of acupuncture are designed to regulate the Qi (pronounced "chee") or energy flow through the meridians (channels of the body). It is believed that by balancing the Qi, blood and meridians disease and pain are eliminated or prevented. Needles are only one method used by acupuncturists. Others include moxibustion, bleeding, cupping massage, and more. **Moxibustion** is the burning of moxa cones near the acupuncture point. This warmth promotes the flow of Qi.

Herbal medicine is linked to acupuncture. There are Qi tonics to increase Qi and promote strength and endurance. There are also Qi herbal plasters to treat sprains, strains, and limb pain. Importantly, there are specific exercise programs such as Tai-ji Quam and Qi-Gong. They help coordinate mind, breath, and movement to balance the flow of Qi.

An acupoint helpful to hikers is Zu San Li, which literally means "foot three miles." This point is in the lower leg, just below where the patella tendon inserts into the shin and just lateral to it. Moxibustion applied daily to this point promotes health, longevity, and strength. It is useful for strained and painful muscles. The easiest way to do this is to burn a moxa stick and hold it over the acupoint 5 to 10 minutes until it warms up. One can also apply deep pressure to this point to alleviate pain.

REFLEXOLOGY

Reflexology is a hands-on technique that manipulates specific reflex points on the feet to bring about, in the words of its proponents, "physiological normalization and vitality of the total body." With the application of touch and pressure to the feet, messages are sent to the brain eliciting a physical response.

Reflexology is a noninvasive and safe alternative medicine therapy. It is not a panacea, but it is a useful adjunct to medicine and should be regarded as such. As medicine becomes more high-tech, the value of "high-touch" treatments becomes apparent.

Reflexology on the Trail

To employ a simple reflexology technique to relax sore feet, look for a surface to stand on to stimulate the reflexes—small pebbles are ideal. Take off your shoes, stand comfortably with feet side-by-side, and start rolling back on your heels, then forward onto the sole, ball of the foot, and finally rocking up on your toes, then slowly reversing back to the heels. Continue this for a few minutes.

For relaxation and pain reduction, sit comfortably and apply a tiny amount of lotion. Take one foot with both hands, and with a wringing motion start above the ankle and slowly "wring" the area down to the toes. Repeat this three or four times. Of course, using this technique with the help of your significant other is even more appealing.

For pain around the spine, sit comfortably, invert the left foot with your left hand. "Walk" your right thumb up the medial (big toe) side of the left foot. To do this, press firmly at the base of the medial heel and move towards the toes in one-quarter-inch sections. When you get to the big toe, reverse direction and walk back to the heel. Repeat this three or four times and then switch to the other foot.

For hip, back, and sciatica pain, again sit comfortably, press firmly on the lateral (fifth toe) side of the right foot following the outline of the ankle with the right thumb. Repeat three or four times and then switch to the other foot. For knee and leg pain, look for the cuboid notch on the lateral side of the right heel. Press firmly with the right index finger to cover the triangle there. Repeat and then switch to the other foot. To relax breathing, press firmly on the plantar (sole) surface of one foot along the ridge of the ball of the foot starting by the fifth toe. Slowly work your way medially towards the big toe and work your way back. Repeat, and then switch to the other foot.

All these treatments are excellent after a long hike to relax tired, aching feet.

Stress is a reaction to an adverse stimulus—physical, mental, emotional, internal, or external that tends to disturb the **homeostasis** of an organism—the body's ability to regulate itself in order to maintain function. Stress is necessary for survival, but our society produces excess stress that is difficult to dissipate. Reflexology reduces stress and tension and improves circulation.

There are many reasons to visit a reflexologist. Hikers seek pain relief in the feet, legs, back, or neck. Others may be suffering from stress-related anxiety, sleeplessness, headaches, or chronic pain.

OTHER HEALTH CONCERNS

PREGNANCY

Pregnancy alters your entire physiology. There are nutritional changes, cardiovascular changes, and hormonal changes. However, regular exercise is still encouraged for the mother-to-be, and hiking is a wonderful way to keep active. What you need to avoid is high-impact and exceptionally taxing exercise. A good guideline for your maximum heart rate is 140, but you should discuss this with your doctor before exercise. There are certain contraindications to hiking while pregnant that should also be discussed with your doctor, such as cardiac disease, hypertension, phlebitis, multiple gestation, uterine bleeding, incompetent cervix, fetal problems, etc.

Good common sense indicates not traveling in dangerous areas, avoiding risk of falling, not hiking alone, avoiding extremes of exertion and temperature, taking enough calories and fluids along for you and the baby, and choosing your trails with forethought.

How late in the pregnancy can you continue to hike? That is a personal and medical issue between you and your doctor. Postpartum exercise can begin after a week or two with a vaginal delivery, but wait at least four to six weeks after a C-section and secure your surgeon's OK.

One component of pregnancy that becomes apparent especially during the last trimester and directly affects walking is ligamentous laxity. Hormones are produced that "soften" all the ligaments in the body to allow for delivery of the baby. Feet actually stretch and flatten, and all the supporting ligaments of the leg become more "stretchy," reducing their ability to control joint movement. This is not a time when you can afford to trip and fall, making your trail choice more important. Stay on better-groomed trails, avoid slippery rocks and significant climbing, and wear supportive boots. Certainly your center of balance shifts as the baby develops. Your footing will not be as stable in the last trimester. When you come to that small stream in the path, I hope you don't plan to jump across it.

CHILD-SPECIFIC HIKING PROBLEMS

Within reason, it is never too early to expose your children to nature. Hiking teaches them to appreciate the value of the great outdoors, and they become better people for their involvement in hiking.

Kids go hiking one of three ways: on your back as a baby, as a toddler sometimes on your back, and as an independent walker. Very young infants may be safer in a soft pack on your front. This shifts your center of gravity and puts pressure on your back. As the child ages, he or she should ride on your back, where your pelvis supplies most of the support.

Children are more flexible, adapt better to uneven terrain, and heal more quickly than adults—which is good because they are also more fearless. What benefits they have are made up for by lack of experience and judgment. It should be clear from this book that hiking is not without danger, and when hiking, children should be supervised and instructed. Take some binoculars with you and perhaps a nature book on plants, bugs, birds, etc., and you will find they will eat up this information. They will gain self-confidence, judgment, and common sense by watching you, and they will have fun at the same time.

Children do have one weak point: the growth plates in their bones. The **epiphyseal plate** is the area of a bone from which it grows. It is cartilagenous and is the weak link in the bone. Injuries to the growth plate can cause permanent problems such as a limb length discrepancy. Since it is impossible to tell if a growth plate is injured in the field, a podiatrist or orthopedist should follow up any significant injury. Common sites for growth plate injuries include the knee, lateral foot, Achilles tendon area, and hip joint area.

A child who complains of chronic pain when walking may have one of the following osteochondroses disorders. These are a vascular necrosis, and their cause is unknown. What is known is that there is a temporary disruption in the blood supply to certain areas in the bone, leading to loss of bone and cartilage. While the area ultimately revascularizes and heals, it is long-term process, taking two or more years.

Other childhood osteochondroses include chronic hip pain, especially in 5–10-year-olds, (Legg Calve Perthes disease), chronic knee pain in the 10–15-year-old (Osgood-Schlatters disease), chronic heel pain in the 10–14-year-old (Seevers disease), and chronic foot pain in the 3–5-year-old (Kohler's disease), all of which are more common in boys. Osgood-Schlatters disease is a common cause of knee pain in active adolescents. Downhill hiking is especially taxing on the quadriceps muscle, and its insertion into the tibia can get inflamed, causing pain just below the front of the knee. Pain, tenderness, and swelling in this area are signs of Osgood-Schlatters. It is diagnosed clinically and with X-rays. It is treated with rest, ice, and quadriceps-strengthening exercises. Heel lifts and stretching exercises are useful for Seevers disease, and orthotics may help with Kohler's disease. OTC NSAIDS such as Advil (use careful, in asthmatics) and ice will help for acute pain.

Kids occasionally complain of vague aches in their legs. These are often diagnosed as "growing pains" and as such are ignored. They can be worst at night, especially after a long hike. Growing pains are not normal and are not even related to growing. Yet this phenomenon often occurs in children age 3 to 12. There are a great many guesses as to their cause. They include infectious diseases, damp weather, psychoneurotic rheumatism, sleep disorders, and genetics, but most likely they result from a myositis due to overexertion—basically a muscle strain. Kids run around a lot! On the trail, they could be miles ahead of you if left to their own devices. There is some truth to the belief that during a growth spurt the long bones in the leg may temporarily outgrow the muscles, making them short in comparison, but this is easily checked in a physical exam. Of course, a physician should rule out uncommon causes of limb pain such as stress fractures and juvenile rheumatoid arthritis. Treatment consists of stretching, ice, massage (especially at night), topical pain relievers (such as Ben-Gay), and aspirin. If there is a biomechanical reason, such as excessively flat feet or knock-kneed legs, an orthotic device may be helpful.

SENIOR-SPECIFIC HIKING PROBLEMS

There is no upper age limit for hiking. Hiking provides a great many benefits for the senior citizen. It is a low-impact aerobic exercise for cardiovascular health, and it is the only nonsurgical way to improve circulation to the legs. It has great psychological benefits: exercising and being outdoors improve one's mood, activity keeps your mind clear, and interacting and socializing with other people on a hike is beneficial. It may also seem that as you age, you accumulate limitations—and pain. Well, hiking is a great equalizer; no matter what a person's physical condition, somewhere there is an interesting, beautiful, or challenging walk to take.

There is little doubt that our life expectancy is increasing. This is due to medical advances and lifestyle changes. In fact, once a person reaches 65, their life expectancy if female is 83.6 years and if male is 79.8 years. But there is an important difference between longevity and quality of life. There is also little doubt that profound physiological changes come with age. Starting in the third decade, cardiac output decreases on average six to eight percent per decade, while maximum heart rate decreases by three and two-tenths percent per decade. Maximum oxygen uptake decreases by seven percent per decade. However, this decline is greatly diminished in those individuals with an active lifestyle. Hiking will improve your entire cardiovascular system. Of course, your physician should be consulted before initiating any exercise program.

Other studies indicate that muscle mass peaks in the thirties and plateaus until the fifties. By age 75, individuals have experienced a 25% drop in muscle mass of the legs. Bone mass also peaks in the thirties and diminishes after the forties. There is a significant difference in bone loss between postmenopausal women and men, with men losing one-half percent yearly and women losing two to three percent yearly for at least the first five years postmenopause. It is a proven medical fact that regular exercise builds bone mass. Hiking seniors have more bone density than sedentary seniors. Falls become more serious for the senior citizen. Bones become more brittle and lose their strength. As postmenopausal women develop osteoporosis, fractures become more likely. Consequently, bone density tests have become a commonplace screening exam for women.

Fortunately, common sense can prevent most injuries. Don't overreach a step, make sure the surface of your next step is not slippery, and pay attention to the trail. Why not try a walking stick? It gives you another point of support and may just save you from a fall. It has been demonstrated that exercise improves bone strength. While taking extra calcium is probably a good idea too, it hasn't been shown to be particularly helpful for most people. Women can discuss with their physician hormone replacement therapy, and new prescription medications such as Fosamax, that are quite helpful for osteoporosis.

Senses also diminish with age. Vision and hearing certainly give you clues about your footing and balance while walking on the trail. Another factor is your **proprioception.** This term means the ability of your brain to know what your legs and feet are doing. Stretch receptors in a tendon may report to the brain that there is too much pressure on the tendon and it will tear if the brain doesn't do something about it. If this system is slowed, damage may result.

There are definite changes in articular cartilage in seniors. It is less resilient. It is true that arthritis is unavoidable and that there is no cure. However, prescription medications are very successful in alleviating symptoms, and the key to fighting arthritis is to keep active. Only on the worst of days should you rest a severely inflamed joint. There is also no reason a patient with a replaced hip need stop hiking. Only common sense is needed for their return to the trail. There is no evidence that hiking causes more arthritic changes in the joints. In fact, the opposite has been seen. Except for acute flare-up of arthritis, hiking is very beneficial for the joints. It is sitting in a chair all day that is harmful.

Ligaments and tendons also lose their elasticity, and their ability to rebound from small injuries diminishes. Lack of flexibility is of concern to hikers. People with a diminished range of motion in their joints, inflexible ligaments, and tight muscles are at greater risk of sprains, tendonitis, falls, and even fractures. This is why a stretching program is vital for any senior hiker.

Most seniors' injuries are related to overuse—going too far, too fast. Use common sense when starting a hiking program, and choose your trail with care. Hiking after a heart attack is **not** forbidden. However, the physician must tailor a program to the individual. The goal is to push yourself just a little more each time.

Besides a bypass operation in the leg, there is only one proven way to increase circulation, and that is to walk. If you experience a cramping in your leg while walking that feels better after a minute of rest, that's claudication. It is a message from your muscles that they are not getting enough blood. This can be due to hardening of the arteries. Medications are almost useless, although the prescription drug Trental may help some individuals' symptoms. Remember that walking increases collateral circulation—you actually build new blood vessels around obstructions. To accomplish this, you must walk to the point of cramps, rest one minute, and walk some more. As time goes by, you will find your distance increasing and your cramps diminishing.

You know the saying "use it or lose it"? It applies to loss of bone and muscle very well. Hiking builds up bone and muscle. Sitting in a chair causes them to waste away. So get out there and use it!

HIKING WITH DISABILITIES

The term disability is a politically incorrect word, and rightly so. We all have limitations, some more significant than others. Hiking can "level the playing field." A blind person can hike with a friend or a guide dog, and enjoy the sensations available to them—the sounds, the smells, the textures. An amputee with a prosthetic limb can hike with almost no limitation. New prosthetics are lightweight and biomechanically accurate, and they require significantly less effort to use than did older models. An arthritic person can keep active on the trail. A person with an emotional disorder can seek some peace in nature. A wheelchair-bound person can find a trail that will accommodate the chair—that's hiking. One thing that these limitations necessitate is careful planning. It is even more important to know the trail, take all precautions, bring a friend, know your limits (we all have them), and stay within them. Don't be foolish. Be safe.

The beauty of hiking as a form of exercise is that it is noncontact, noncompetitive, low-impact, and the effort involved is easily controlled by the hiker. Under a physician's care, asthma, diabetes, epilepsy, depression, cardiovascular disease, chronic obstructive pulmonary disease, obesity, and HIV infection are not contraindications to hiking. Common sense indicates that the asthmatic avoids days that are especially cold and dry or polluted, and that they take their inhaler with them. Noninsulin diabetics may actually see a decrease in their need for medications. However, the increased calorie consumption that provides hikers energy may cause diabetics hypoglycemia. They should always carry an emergency glucose supply. The timing of insulin injections should be planned with a physician.

A well-controlled epileptic has virtually no limitations, but common sense dictates against hiking alone. Patients with respiratory problems can increase oxygen consumption with hiking, however the effect is slow—it will take some time to see a difference. You must push yourself just past the point of feeling out of breath. This is conditioning—you must go just beyond your limits each time you hike, and you will see your abilities increase. Those who continue to smoke, however, will not succeed.

SOME FINAL WORDS

The following advice from former patients and fellow hikers may help:

B.D. states that for years, bad bunions stopped her from walking, and she loved to hike. She tried bigger boots, but they caused her foot to slip and created blisters. Pads helped only a little. Her solution—custom-made boots. Sure they are a little expensive, but in allowing her to do the things she enjoyed, the cost was well worth it.

L.J. goes hiking with his autistic son. His son doesn't speak but enjoys walking outdoors. Occasionally, he acts out and screams, but he

Hiking Green

Due to the rapid growth of hiking, many parks and trails get downright crowded. Remember, **we** are the visitors, and it is our job not to disturb the environment. This dictates staying on the trails. Going off a trail increases erosion, soil damage, and loss of vegetation. Deep tread lugs on hiking boots damage the soil. If you use hiking sticks, make sure you use rubber tips and not the trail-damaging metal ones. Don't break off, dig up, or otherwise damage the plants. Take all your trash out, plus one extra piece found along the trail. While you are at it, how about volunteering your time with your local environmental group? Trail maintenance is a group effort and very rewarding.

is quickly calmed by his father. L.J. states that if he plans a short, interesting hike, he knows his son enjoys it, and it gives them an opportunity to be together.

R.B. has severe hip arthritis. He continues to stay active, and hiking is his favorite activity. He relies heavily on his walking stick and stays on well-groomed, not-too-steep trails. He rests on only the really bad days, and he knows that in order to stay active, he has to keep moving. He has planned a hip replacement surgery so that he can continue hiking without pain.

J.F. is blind, but she often goes hiking with her guide dog (a golden retriever) and her boyfriend. She states she is comfortable enough to go with the dog alone, but she is more confident with a friend along. She enjoys the sounds of the birds, the ocean swell, and the smells of nature.

N.D. had a stroke years ago. He is alert but a little unsteady. While he no longer climbs mountains, there are many well-groomed flat trails for him to hike on. He doesn't want to spend the rest of his life in his bedroom. He wants out!

J.P always felt unsteady on his feet. When he was finally diagnosed with Charcot Marie tooth disease, a severe neuromuscular disease, he thought his hiking days were over. He bought himself a very sturdy hiking boot and modified a walking stick to give him more support. His future is unclear, but at least for now, with a little creativity, he is able to climb his favorite mountain again.

P.P. had polio as a child, with a resultant drop foot. When he walked, he dragged his toes because he was unable to lift his foot up. He was fitted with an ankle foot orthotic. This is a plastic device that starts behind the calf, continues down to the foot, and fits inside the boot. It can be hinged with a spring or solid, and it can assist in holding up the foot, allowing a more normal gait. This device allowed him to become an active hiker after decades of sedentary life.

C.R. had a horrible hammertoe and an extremely painful corn on her fifth toe for years. It was so bad it stopped her from hiking. She ultimately had a simple surgical correction of her toe, and she was back hiking comfortably in five weeks.

G.S., like many who feel overwhelmed by the stresses of life, is depressed. She is on one of the popular antidepressant medications— Prozac. There are times when all the joy goes out of her life, and even the things she used to enjoy no longer give her pleasure. Often, she is tired, sleeps poorly, and is irritable. She states that hiking helps clear her mind and stops her from focusing on herself as she enjoys the scenery. The exercise releases her natural endorphins, and she feels better.

R.D. was a chronic smoker who could barely walk up a flight of stairs. He was diagnosed with COPD—chronic obstructive pulmonary disease. He gave up smoking, had a thorough physical, and was approved to begin a walking program. It took over nine months for him to progress from once around the block to a nice two- to three-hour flat hike in a local park. It is his hope to climb some of the local hills, for the challenge and the views.

AFTERWORD

Last fall, I had the pleasure of revisiting my favorite mountain, Mount Monadnock in New Hampshire, a beautiful New England location. It is the most-climbed mountain in the United States, and while it isn't statistically impressive, (3,100 feet elevation), its grandeur, especially in the fall, is unsurpassed. The leaves were every color of the spectrum: green, yellow, orange, red, and brown.

It had been 20 years since my last visit, and I wondered if age and cardiovascular fitness (or lack thereof) would "do me in," so to speak. Climbing the mountain was my goal. Initially, to reach the summit was "to conquer" the mountain. As we climbed, I felt the goal change to "to become one with" the mountain. While I know this may sound corny, initially I struggled, complaining of a pounding heart, but when I found a slow and easy cadence, things felt better. It was like getting in synch with the trail. Going down was completely different. We chose a very rocky trail. Here, the worry was falling and injuring an ankle. It was also very tough on the knees. At first I examined every footfall and felt the tension in my legs holding them rigid to guard against falling. My eyes had to see every rock to insure proper foot placement. Not long into the descent, I again developed a rhythm. My feet found their own safe footholds, and again I felt in synch with the mountain. Since I swim for exercise, I related this to the difference between a comfortable swimmer gliding through the water and a novice, anxious swimmer fighting against the water.

This is not to say that you can ignore good judgement and experience when climbing a mountain, because a mountain can be unforgiving to the foolish. But fighting against the mountain to conquer it is not the same as becoming one with the mountain—that is how a person becomes a hiker.

Appendix

Please note that the following list is included for your information; it is not an endorsement of any product. Nor is any omission an indication of a poor product. You must make your own judgements. There are many other fine products, companies, and information sites not listed. Take advantage of local stores, national companies, your friends, the Internet, etc. to find the best products for your needs. When surfing the net, remember that web addresses come and go rapidly. Most (but not all) information is accurate—you must use your judgement, and check the links that most sites provide.

RUNNING SHOE COMPANIES

Avia	(800) 333-8404	www.aviaselect.com
Asics	(800) 333-8404	www.asicstiger.com
New Balance	(800) 622-1218	www.newbalance.com
Nike	(503) 671-6453	www.nike.com
Reebok	(800) 843-4444	www.reebok.com
Saucony	(800) 365-4933	www.saucony.com

INTERNET SITES

Great Outdoors Recreational Page (GORP)	www.gorp.com
Sierra Club	www.sierraclub.org
All American Hiking and Backpacking Trail Guide	www.aspenserv.com/hiking
Hikenet	www.members.aol.com/hikenet

NEWSGROUPS

rec.backcountry

rec.outdoors

outdoorreview.com/gear

ORGANIZATIONS

American Amputee   (501) 666-2523
   Foundation

American Podiatric   (301) 571-9200   www.apma.org
   Medical Association

American Hiking   (301) 565-6704   www.americanhiking.org
   Association

Arthritis Foundation   (800) 283-7800   www.arthritis.org

National Pedorthic   (800) 803-7813   www.nps-foot.com
   Services

National Women's   (202) 347-1140
   Health Network   www.womenshealthnetwork.com

National Organization (202) 293-5960   www.nod.org
   on Disability

Sportsmedicine.com

HIKING CATALOGS

Campmor   (800) 230-2151   www.campmor.com

Eastern Mountain   (888) 463-6367   www.emsonline.com
   Sports

L.L. Bean   (800) 221-4221   www.llbean.com

REI   (800) 426-4840   www.rei.com

Pedifix   (800) 733-4349

HIKING BOOT INTERNET INFORMATION

www.learn2.com/05/0503/0503.htm

www.snowcounty.com/gear/hike.htm

www.bcexpress.com/boots.htm

www.technicausa.com

www.gearfinder.com

HIKING MEDICAL KITS

www.adventurenetwork.com/health

www.chinookmed.com (800) 766-1365

www.atwatercarey.com (800) 359-1646

Adventure Medical kits (800) 324-3517

HIKING LOCATIONS

www.trailweb.com

www.trailworks.com

www.greatoutdoors.com

www.trailsource.com

www.outdoorplaces.com

BOOT MANUFACTURERS

Adidas	(800) 677-6638	www.adidas.com
AKU	(888) 258-2668	www.aku.it
Alpina Sports Corp	(603) 448-3101	www.alpinasports.com
Asolo	(800) 879-4644	www.asolo.com
Boreal	(949) 498-1011	www.borealusa.com
Cabela's Inc.	(800) 234-4444	www.cabelas.com
Danner	(800) 345-0430	www.danner.com
Dunham Bootmakers	(800) 843-2668	www.dunhambootmakers.com
Eastern Mountain Sports		(603) 924-9571 www.emsonline.com
Five Ten Co.	(909) 798-4222	www.fiveten.com
Garmont	(888) 343-5200	www.garmont.com

Gore-Tex	(800) 431-GORE	
Gronell	(250) 785-0707	www.gronell.com
Hi-Tec	(800) 521-1698	www.hi-tec.com
Kamik	(514) 341-3950	www.kamik.com
Kayland	(514) 871-0771	www.kayland.com
La Fuma	(303) 527-140	www.lafuma.com
La Spotiva USA	(303) 443-8710	www.sportiva.com
Limmer Boots	(603) 694-2668	www.limmerboot.com
L.L. Bean	(800) 809-7057	www.llbean.com
Lowa Boots	(203) 353-0116	www.lowaboots.com
Merrel	(800) 869-3348	www.merrellboot.com
Montrail	(800) 647-0224	www.montrail.com
Nike ACG		www.nike.com
Nordica	(800) 291-5800	www.nordica.com
One Sport	(206) 621-9303	
Raichle	(800) 431-2204	www.raichle.com
REI	(800) 426-4840	www.rei.com
Salomon	(800) 995-3556	www.salomon-sports.com
Scarpa	(801) 278-5533	www.scarpa-us.com
Technica	(603) 298-8032	technicausa.com
Teva	(800) 367-8382	www.teva.com
The North Face	(800) 535-3331	www.thenorthface.com
Timberland	(800) 258-0855	www.timberland.com
Trezeta America	(877) 873-9382	www.trezeta.com
Trukke Winter Sports	(888) 387-8553	www.trukke.com
Vasque	(800) 224-4453	www.vasque.com
Wolverine Boots	(888) 927-9675	www.wolverineboots andshoes.com
Vibram	(800) VIBRAM7	

BOOT RESOLERS

Barlow's Boots	(315) 363-6353 or (315) 691-6574	
The Cobbler & Cordwainer	(800) 788-2668	www.cobcord.com
The Custom Foot	(303) 761-4002	
Dave Page, Cobbler	(800) 252-1229	www.davepagecobbler.com
Down East Service Center	(212) 925-2632	
Komito Boots	(800) 422-2668	
Mekan Boot Co.	(800) 657-2884	
Mountain Soles Boot Repair	(503) 236-0785	www.mtnsoles.com
Progressive Outdoor Footwear Repair	(800) 783-7764	
Resole America	(888) 349-7463	www.resole.com
Rocky Mountain Resole	(800) 228-2668	www.rmresole.com
Wilson's Eastside Sports	(760) 873-7520	

HIKING MAGAZINES

Backpacker Magazine	(800) 666-3434	www.bpbascecamp.com
Stride Magazine	(612) 844-0512	www.stridemag.com
Outside Magazine	(505) 989-7100	www.outsidemag.com

WILDERNESS TRAINING

Wilderness Medicine Institute	(970) 641-3572	www.wmi.nols.edu
Sirius	(514) 982-0066	siriusmed.com
SOLO	(603) 447-6711	

COMPANY PRODUCTS

Aircast	(800) 526 8785
Beiersdorf	(800) 221 7573
Biofreeze	(800) 246 3733
Chopat	(800) 221 1601
Gordon labs	(800) 356 7870
Implus	(800) 446 7587
Orthomedics	(800) 733 6999
Pedinol	(800) 733 4665
Silipos	(800) 229 4404
Sorbothane	(800) 992 6594
Spenco	(800) 877 3626
Viscolas heel	(423) 265 4030

GPS TRACKING

Magellan	(800) 707-7840	magellandis.com
Garmin		Garmin.com

SOCK MANUFACTURERS

Acorn Socks		www.acornearth.com
Bridgedale	0116 234 4646	www.bridgedale-socks.co.uk
Columbia Sports wear		www.columbia.com
Dahlgren Footwear	(800) 635-8539	www.dahlgrenfootwear.com
Fox River		www.foxrivermills.com
Patagonia	(800) 638-6464	www.patagonia.com
Smartwool	(800) 550-9665	www.smartwool.com
Socksappeal.com		
Thorlo	(800) 438 0209	www.thorlo.com
Timberland		www.timberland.com
Wigwam		www.wigwam.com
Woolrich	(800) 995-1299	www.woolrich.com

Index

Proprioception, in elderly persons, 160
Prosthetic limb, hiking with, 161
Psoriasis, 86–87
Psoriatic arthritis, 97
Pulse rate, targets for, in exercise, 52–53
Pump bump, 132
Puncture wounds, 79

Quadriceps
    strengthening exercises for, 61
    trigger points in, 94

Rabies, prevention of, 112
Rain, 68
Rashes, 86, 102–3
Raynaud's disease, 82
Reflexology, 153–55
Relaxation, reflexology for, 154
Respiratory disorders, hiking with, 162, 164–65
Rheumatoid arthritis, 96
R.I.C.E. protocol, 90
Rocks
    scrambling over, 71–72
    in stream crossings, 70–71
Rocky Mountain spotted fever, 108–10
Runner's knee, 140

Scabies, 106–8
Sciatica, 148, 150, 154
Scorpion stings, 105
Seasons, extremes in, 68
Seniors, hiking problems in, 158–61
Sesamoids, 125
Severs disease, 157
Shin splints, 60–61, 147–48
Shock, in snake bite, 112
Shoes. *See also* Boots
    inserts for, 42–44
    running, manufacturers of, 167
Skin injuries and disorders, 77–88
    alternative remedies for, 151–52
    blisters, 64, 114–15
    burns, 77–78
    calluses, 64, 118–20
    corns, 64, 118–20
    cuts, 78–80
    frostbite, 80–83
    fungal infections, 85–86, 113–14
    insect bites and stings, 103–10

from plants, 102–3
psoriasis, 86–87
rashes, 86, 102–3
Raynaud's disease, 82
sunburn, 66, 83–85
in varicose veins, 146–47
warts, 87–88
Snake bites, 110–12
Snow, hiking in, 73–74
Socks, 22–28
    construction of, 25–27
    fit of, 26, 27
    hydrophilic or hydrophobic, 22
    length of, 26
    liners for, 27
    manufacturers of, 173
    materials for, 22–25
    padding of, 25
    seamless, 25
    warming devices in, 27–28
    for winter, 73
Spider bites, 105
Spinal disorders, 148–51
Sprains, 90–91, 135–39
Spurs
    heel, 129–31
    toes, 124
Stamina. *See* Fitness and stamina
Standing back stretch exercise, 62
Stings, insect, 103–10
Stockings, support, for varicose veins, 146
Strengthening exercises
    anterior tibial, 60–61
    for iliotibial band syndrome, 143–44
    myths about, 57
    quadriceps, 61
Stress, reflexology for, 155
Stress fractures, 88–89
Stretching exercises
    for back, 62–63, 150
    benefits of, 56
    for calf, 59–60
    for cramps, 93
    for hamstrings, 57–59
    for iliotibial band syndrome, 143
    method for, 56–57
    for trigger points, 94–96
Styloid process, irritation of, 134
Subtalar joint, biomechanics of, 12–13
Summer weather, hazards of, 74

About the Author

A native of New York, **Dr. Stuart Plotkin** (shown here with daughter Paula) began hiking in the Adirondacks at the age of 13. Since then, he has hiked extensively throughout the United States, including jaunts through Yosemite, Mt. Ranier, the Grand Canyon, and the White Mountains. A graduate of the California College of Podiatric Medicine and a diplomate of the American Board of Podiatric Orthopedics, Dr. Plotkin currently practices podiatry on Long Island. These days, most of Dr. Plotkin's hiking occurs in Montana, Wyoming, and Alberta—dinosaur country—where he helps collect fossils for various natural history museums. Though he's had his share of blisters, shin splints, poison ivy, and bugs, Dr. Plotkin still enjoys a good hike in the woods. He has written various technical journal articles; *The Hiking Engine* is his first book.